The
Quarantine Cookbook

Beth Carter

Award-Winning Author

To my younger brother, Steve, who has been a flight nurse for nearly three decades. He has always been on the front line of healthcare emergencies. We're so proud of you.

And to every healthcare hero who bravely and skillfully cared for COVID-19 patients. Also, much gratitude to first responders, the military, businesses who quickly retrofitted their companies to manufacture much-needed Personal Protective Equipment, and to the many individuals who stepped up during this crisis—many of whom are making homemade masks, applauding healthcare workers, and showing love in a variety of heartfelt ways.

Last but definitely not least, to my dear, departed grandmother, Evelyn, who cooked by profession at an elementary school, hospital cafeteria, and was head chef at the Aurora Senior Citizen Center where locals always lined up on fried chicken and meatloaf days! You and my superior pie-making mom, Carol, both inspired me to cook. Thank you.

Table of Contents

Introduction

"If you're going through hell, keep going."
Winston Churchill

Isn't this the perfect quote during a pandemic? I don't remember a time as frightening as this, and I'm sure none of us had ever heard the terms social distancing or flattening the curve before this horrendous virus called COVID-19 caught everyone off guard. I think of Coronavirus as an invisible monster lurking behind every corner, seemingly worldwide. As I'm sure you can relate, the virus gave me pause, anxiety, concern, and non-stop worry. Finding myself unable to work on my next novel since I often write humorous women's fiction and romantic comedy, I turned to this project since my funny muse was hiding under the bed.

After watching non-stop news and briefings, I observed wonderful people who rose above the crisis making home-made masks, delivering food to healthcare workers, and creating colorful posters for nursing home residents or family members.

Since I can barely sew on a button but wanted to contribute *something* positive during this scary time, I found myself cooking nightly and often posted pictures online. After receiving several requests for the recipes and hearing that my posts were inspiring and giving others ideas for meal planning, I came up with my quarantine project, and this cookbook was born.

Many of these recipes have been family favorites for decades. I hope you enjoy the recipes I've included, many of which have five or fewer ingredients, which is easy on the pantry and budget. Some recipes are low-fat and low-sugar. I have hypoglycemia, so I always opt for low or no-sugar recipes but you can use sugar if desired. There's also plenty of comfort food which is a necessity during trying times.

In addition, I added nearly sixty Non-Stir Crazy Activities, unique Six-Word Memoirs on Quarantine Life, and funny quotes about food. I worked in healthcare marketing for a decade and learned humor is important for our mental health.

During this crisis, as everyone knows, restaurant dining was no longer an option. We've made friends with many servers, chefs, bartenders, and restaurant owners all over town. My heart broke for them as they shuttered their doors and furloughed employees. Schools closed which meant many parents were thrust into homeschooling. That didn't affect us but I can only imagine how challenging it was to relearn math. Insert bug-egged emoticon here!

More frivolous, but much-enjoyed services, like hair and nail salons were also out of the question. Currently, my hair is akin to Phyllis Diller's. Remember her? Not that old? Google her name.

I could go on and on, but I'm sure you're well aware of the lost jobs, services, and ensuing heartbreak. My heart goes out to all of the healthcare heroes and families who have lost loved ones to this vicious virus. Much gratitude goes to all medical professionals, truck drivers, grocers, postal workers, first responders, and everyone else who kept this country running during this surreal crisis.

Back to this book. I'm a cookbook-collecting nerd, so it makes sense that I'd eventually create one of my own. Inside THE QUARANTINE COOKBOOK, you'll find recipes for appetizers, salads, soups, side dishes, entrees, meatless meals, and desserts. Mix and match dishes from these sections, and you'll have menu ideas for weeks.

Please share photos of the recipes you use and post pictures with the hashtag

#TheQuarantineCookbook or **#thequarantinecookbook**.

Let's start cooking. Stay healthy and happy eating!

www.bethcarter.com

Appetizers & Snacks

Bacon-Wrapped Onion Rings

Frozen onion rings

Bacon

Preheat oven to 375 degrees. Wrap bacon around onion rings; overlap the bacon. Place on a cookie sheet and bake for 15 minutes. Serve with ranch dip or catsup.

Brenda's Cheeseball

1 jar pimento cheese spread

2 jars Old English cheese spread

6-8 oz. cream cheese (may use fat-free)

1-2 tsp. onion, minced small

5-6 drops Worcestershire sauce

½ - 1 cup pecans, crushed

Soften cream cheese. Mix with cheese spread in a bowl. Add onion and Worcestershire sauce. Refrigerate approximately 20 minutes to handle. Shape into a ball and roll in crushed pecans.

Note: This may also be placed in a small serving bowl. Sprinkle top with pecans. Serves: 8-10

Crockpot Hot Artichoke Dip

2 14 oz. jars marinated artichoke hearts, drained

1 cup mayonnaise

1 cup sour cream

1 cup water chestnuts, chopped

2 cups grated parmesan cheese

¼ cup scallions, chopped (may substitute onion salt)

Cut artichoke hearts into half-inch pieces. And mayonnaise, sour cream, water chestnuts, and parmesan cheese. Stir well and place in a slow cooker.

Cook on high one to 2 hours or on low 3-4 hours. This is an easy, delicious dip! Serve with crackers, chips, or even cucumber slices.

Serves: 6-8

"The secret of success in life is to eat what you like and let the food fight it out inside." Mark Twain

Curry Dip

1 cup Mayonnaise (may use less fat)

1 tsp. Garlic salt

1 tsp. Onion powder

1 tsp. Horseradish

1 tsp. Curry powder

1 tsp. Tarragon vinegar

Combine all ingredients and mix in a bowl. Place in refrigerator and chill at least eight hours. Serve with crackers or vegetables.

Easy Cream Cheese Appetizer

One block of cream cheese (may use low-fat or fat-free)

½ jar of any jelly or preserves: Jalapeno Apple, Red Hot Pepper Jelly, or whatever is in your pantry.

Place cream cheese on a plate. Top with jelly/preserves and serve with crackers. Simple and easy!

Hummus & Veggies

1 7 oz. container original hummus

¼ cup red onion, chopped

1 ripe tomato, chopped

½ cucumber, peeled and chopped

¼ cup feta cheese

Spread hummus onto a serving plate. Top with vegetables.
Finish with cheese. Serve with crackers.

Serves: 4-6

Jarlsberg Cheese Dip

2 cups chopped onions

2 cups mayonnaise

2 cups Jarlsberg cheese, shredded

Preheat oven to 350 degrees. Mix all ingredients together. Bake in a glass dish for 20 minutes. Refrigerate leftovers. May reheat in microwave or slow cooker. Serve with crackers or vegetables.

"An onion can make people cry, but there has never been a vegetable invented to make them laugh." Will Rogers

Kale Chips

Bunch Kale

Sea salt

Preheat oven to 350 degrees. Wash and separate kale into large bite-sized pieces. Dry on a paper towel. Place on a cookie sheet, spray with cooking spray, and top with sea salt. Bake for 20-30 minutes.

Serves: 2-4

"You've got bad eating habits if you use a grocery cart in a 7-Eleven, OK?" Dennis Miller

Pantry Snack Mix

6 cups Chex cereal or Cheerios

1 cup goldfish

1 cup pretzels

1 cup cashews, peanuts or almonds

6 tablespoons butter, melted

2 tablespoons Worcestershire sauce

1 tsp. seasoning salt

½ tsp. garlic powder

1 tsp. onion salt or onion powder

Place dry ingredients in slow cooker. Combine butter, Worcestershire sauce, and seasonings. Pour over dry ingredients and mix well. Cook on low 2 hours, stirring every 30 minutes.

This recipe uses many items from your pantry. Mix and match using whatever dry pantry items you have on hand. Keep leftovers in a covered container.

Serves: 10

Party Dip

1-1/2 cups mayo (may use low fat)

1 cup sour cream (again, low-fat is fine)

2 cups mozzarella, shredded

¼ cup parmesan cheese

1 tsp. garlic powder

Add all ingredients in a bowl. Refrigerate a few hours or overnight. Serve with cut veggies or crackers.

Serves: 6

Pepper Jelly Cheeseball

1 cup cheddar cheese, shredded

1 cup pecans, chopped

½ cup green onions, chopped

½ cup cream cheese (fat-free or low-fat is fine)

½ cup Pepper Jelly

Combine cheese, pecans, onions, and cream cheese. Flatten on a serving plate and chill a few hours. Spoon jelly over top and serve with crackers.

Roquefort & Sherry Dip

One package Roquefort

2 packages cream cheese (may use low or fat-free)

Sherry

Let cheeses soften. Add Sherry until softened to desired consistency. Stir and place in a bowl. Great with crackers, chips, or veggies. Refrigerate leftovers.

Serves: 4

Salmon Cheese Spread

6 to 8 oz. cream cheese, softened (fat free is fine)

3 T. mayonnaise (may use low-fat mayo)

1 T. lemon juice

½ tsp. salt

½ tsp. curry powder

½ tsp. dried basil

¼ tsp. pepper

1 7.5 oz. can salmon, drained

2-3 green onions, chopped

Crackers (for serving)

In a bowl, combine the cream cheese, mayo, and lemon juice. Add salt, curry powder, basil, and pepper. Mix well and gently stir in salmon and onions.

Cover and refrigerate for 1-2 hours or overnight. Serve with crackers.

Serves: 4

Sausage Balls

½ package mild or hot sausage (in a roll)

1 cup Bisquick

1 cup cheddar cheese, shredded

Preheat oven to 375 degrees. Place all three ingredients in a large bowl, crumbling sausage. Mix well with a wooden spoon until blended. Roll sausage mixture into 2-inch balls.

Spray a broiler pan with cooking spray. Bake for 20 minutes. These are delicious! I remember making them for my parents' 25th wedding anniversary. They just celebrated their 63rd!

Yield: 12-16 balls

Strawberry Cheese Appetizer

1 cup grated cheddar cheese

1 cup chopped pecans

2 green onions, chopped

1 cup light or regular mayo

1 5-oz. jar strawberry preserves (may use sugar-free)

Crackers

Combine cheese, pecans, onions, and mayonnaise. Mix until blended. Spread mixture on a serving platter. Top with strawberry preserves. Serve with crackers. This is a beautiful, unique appetizer.

Serves: 10

Tex Mex Dip

First layer:

2 cans bean dip

Second layer:

3 avocados, diced

2 T. lemon juice

½ tsp. salt

¼ tsp. pepper

Third layer:

1 cup sour cream (fat-free is fine)

½ cup low-fat mayonnaise

1 pkg. taco seasoning

Fourth layer:

Green onions, chopped (including tops)

2-3 tomatoes, seeded and chopped

8 oz. shredded cheddar cheese

Prepare each layer as described above, beginning with the bean dip on the bottom of a large serving platter. A cheat for the second layer: Simply use already prepared guacamole!

Once all four layers are prepared, serve immediately with taco or corn chips or store in the refrigerator. This is delicious and well worth the effort!

Serves 10-12

Turkey Cranberry Sliders

8 ounces deli Turkey (or ham)

4 slices of either: Gouda, Swiss, or Provolone cheese

1 cup cranberry relish

1 pkg. Hawaiian dinner rolls (12 rolls)

3 T. butter

1 tsp. Worcestershire sauce

1 ½ teaspoons Dijon mustard

½ tsp. everything bagel seasoning (or poppy seeds)

Preheat oven to 375. Spray a 9 by 13 baking dish with cooking spray. Slice buns in half. Remove the top buns and set aside. Place the bottom half of the bun in a pan.

Add the turkey, top with cranberry relish, and slices of cheese. Place the top of the bun over each.

In a small microwave safe bowl, mix the butter, Worcestershire sauce, Dijon mustard, and seasoning. Microwave for 30-60 seconds until butter is melted. Brush mixture atop the buns. Cover with foil and bake for 15 minutes.

These are amazing! I spoke to a book club in Florida last year and the coordinator served these.

Quarantine Snack Mix

6 cups caramel corn

2 cups cashews (peanuts or almonds)

1 1/2 cups M & M's (or whatever candy you have)

1/2 cup raisins

Combine all ingredients in a large ball. This snack mix may be varied in the fall with candy corn. Then, it becomes a Halloween Snack Mix! It's colorful, easy, and delicious. Feel free to change it up.

Serves: 8 to 10

Breads

Cake Mix Banana Bread

1 package yellow cake mix

1 cup ripe banana, mashed

½ cup buttermilk

1/3 cup vegetable or canola oil

3 eggs, whisked

1 cup pecans or walnuts, chopped (optional)

Preheat oven to 350 degrees. Grease two loaf pans. Beat all ingredients in large bowl on low speed for 30 seconds. Then switch to medium speed and beat two minutes longer.

Bake 30-35 minutes until toothpick comes out clean. Cool completely and remove from pans.

Confetti Bubble Ring

4 slices bacon, cooked and crumbled

1 8 oz. can biscuits

1/3 cup butter, melted

1 T. pimiento

1/3 cup green peppers, chopped

1/3 cup onions, chopped

1/3 cup parmesan cheese or cheddar cheese

Prepare bacon in skillet or microwave. Let cool. Preheat oven to 400 degrees.

Cut biscuits into quarters. In a mixing bowl combine remaining ingredients, mixing lightly. Add crumbled bacon. Pour all into a greased Bundt pan.

Bake for 20 minutes or until a toothpick inserted is clean.

Serve with your favorite Italian meal.

Serves: 8

Cranberry Pumpkin Bread

2 eggs, whisked

2 cups sugar (Splenda may be substituted)

½ cup canola or vegetable oil

1 cup pumpkin (pie filling)

2 ¼ cups all-purpose flour

1 T. pumpkin pie spice

1 tsp. baking soda

½ tsp. salt

1 cup cranberries, chopped

Preheat oven to 350 degrees. Grease two loaf pans.

Combine eggs, sugar, oil, and pumpkin. Mix well. In a separate bowl, combine flour, pie spice, soda, and salt. Make a well in the center. Pour pumpkin mixture into the well. Stir until dry ingredients are moistened. Fold in cranberries.

Bake at 350 degrees for one hour.

Yield: 2 loaves (freezes well)

Fruity Coffeecake

1 package white or French vanilla cake mix

½ cup sour cream (may use low-fat)

1/3 cup butter, melted

2 eggs

1 tsp. vanilla

1 can pie filling (cherry, blueberry, or peach)

Preheat oven to 350. Stir all ingredients except the pie filling in a large bowl. Reserve one cup of the dough.

Spread dough mixture in pan. Top with the pie filling. Using a spoon, drop reserved dough on top of the pie filling.

Bake 25-29 minutes until a toothpick comes out clean. Let cool.

Glaze:

1 cup powdered sugar

2 T. milk

½ tsp. vanilla

Mix powdered sugar and milk until smooth. Add vanilla and stir. If too thick, add more milk. If too thin, add more powdered sugar. Serves: 12

Mexican Cornbread

1 can creamed corn

1 cup yellow cornmeal

¾ cup milk

1/3 cup vegetable or canola oil

2 eggs, slightly beaten

1 tsp. baking powder

½ tsp. salt

4 ounces chopped green chilies (mild or medium)

1 cup shredded cheddar cheese

Preheat oven to 375 degrees. Blend all ingredients except chiles and cheese. Pour half of the batter into a 9 by 13 pan. Sprinkle with cheddar cheese and peppers. Top with remaining batter. Bake for 35 to 40 minutes.

This bread is delicious with any kind of soup, salad, or entree!

Serves: 8-10

Pumpkin Bread

4 eggs

1 cup vegetable or canola oil

2 cups sugar (may use Splenda)

15 oz. can pumpkin

2 cups flour

2 tsp. baking powder

1 tsp. soda

½ tsp. salt

2 tsp. cinnamon

½ tsp. ginger

½ tsp. cloves

½ tsp. nutmeg

Preheat oven to 350 degrees. In a large bowl, blend eggs, oil, sugar, and pumpkin. In a separate bowl, combine flour, baking powder, soda, salt, and spices. Mix well and stir into egg mixture. Beat on medium speed for 2 minutes. Pour into a greased 9 x 13 pan. Bake for 20-25 minutes and cool.

Frosting:

6 oz. cream cheese (fat-free works)

½ c butter, melted

1 ½ T. milk

1 tsp. vanilla

3 cups powdered sugar

Mix well and spread over cake. Store in refrigerator.

Quick Herb Bread

3 cups all-purpose flour

3 T. sugar

1 T. baking powder

½ tsp. salt

½ tsp. ground nutmeg

3 tsp. caraway seeds

½ tsp. dried thyme

1 egg

1 cup milk (skim or not)

1/3 cup canola oil

Preheat oven to 350 degrees. In a large bowl, whisk the first seven ingredients. In a smaller bowl, mix egg, milk, and oil until blended. Add to flour mixture until moistened.

Place in a greased loaf pan and bake 40-50 minutes (until a toothpick comes out clean.) Cool several minutes before removing from pan.

Delicious with soup or salad, and no yeast is needed!

Zucchini Bread

3 cups flour, sifted

3 eggs

1 cup vegetable or canola oil

2 cups sugar

2 cups zucchini, peeled and grated

2 tsp. vanilla

1 tsp. teaspoon salt

1 tsp. baking soda

¼ tsp. baking powder

3 tsp. cinnamon

½ cup pecans or walnuts, optional

Preheat oven to 325 degrees. In a large bowl, beat eggs until foamy. Add oil, sugar, zucchini, and vanilla. Sift dry ingredients and add to egg mixture. Stir until blended. Add nuts if desired.

Pour into two greased loaf pans and bake for 50 minutes. After cooling, one loaf may be frozen.

Yield: 2 loaves

Salads

Asian Cole Slaw

1 package coleslaw

1 4 oz. package sunflower seeds

4 oz. sliced almonds or cashews

1 pkg. beef Ramen noodles, crunched inside bag

½ cup vegetable or canola oil

2 T. sugar or Splenda

3 T. white vinegar or red wine vinegar

Seasoning packet from Ramen noodles

2-3 green onions, chopped

Place coleslaw, sunflower seeds, nuts, and noodles in large bowl. Separately, whisk vegetable oil, sugar, vinegar, and seasoning packet. Pour liquid mixture over the coleslaw mix and toss well. Refrigerate before serving. Will keep for 4-5 days.

This has been a must-have salad at our family dinners for decades!

Serves: 6

Bacon and Chive Potato Salad

6 cups small red potatoes, unpeeled and quartered

½ cup real mayonnaise

2 T. ground mustard

8 slices bacon, cooked and crumbled

¼ cup chives, chopped (or use green onions or scallions)

Add quartered potatoes to boiling water. Cook 15 minutes or until fork tender. Drain. In a large bowl, mix mayonnaise and mustard. Add cooked potatoes, bacon, and chives/onions. Stir until coated. Refrigerate until serving.

Serves: 6-8

"People want honest, flavourful food, not some show-off meal that takes days to prepare." Ted Allen

Canned Fruit Salad

1 jar maraschino cherries, drained

1 can pineapple tidbits, drained (drink the juice!)

1 can mandarin oranges, drained

1 can sliced peaches, drained

1 can apricot pie filling

3 bananas, sliced (optional)

Combine all into a bowl. Mix, chill, and enjoy! This is handy during quarantine because we all run out of fresh produce.

Cherry Fluff Salad

1 can cherry pie filling

1 small can crushed pineapple, drained

1 can Eagle Brand milk

1 container Cool Whip

½ cup crushed pecans

Combine cherries and canned milk. Add drained pineapple. Spoon in Cool Whip and pecans. Chill a few hours or overnight. This is an easy, pretty salad which could also serve as a dessert. Just put it in pretty parfait glasses or glass bowls.

Serves: 8 to 10

Five-Cup Salad

1 cup marshmallows

1 cup mandarin oranges, drained

1 cup pineapple, drained

1 cup sour cream (I use fat-free)

1 cup coconut

Combine all ingredients in a bowl and refrigerate a few hours or overnight. Just like its name, there's one cup of everything!

Green Salad with Mandarin Oranges

1 bag salad greens

1 small can Mandarin oranges, drained

2-3 green onions (or ½ red onion), chopped

1 avocado, sliced (optional)

½ cup dried cherries or cranberries

Balsamic dressing

Add salad greens to a large bowl. Prepare fruit and vegetables. Stir into salad mix. Before serving, add dressing.

Serves: 4-6

Green Salad with Strawberries

1 bag salad greens

6-8 strawberries, sliced

2-3 green onions, chopped

1 avocado, sliced

¼ cup pecans or sunflower seeds

Balsamic dressing

Add salad greens to a large bowl. Prepare fruit and vegetables. Stir into salad mix with nuts. Before serving, add dressing. Serves: 4-6

Italian Pasta Salad

1 package spiral pasta, cooked and drained

1 green pepper, chopped

1 red pepper, chopped

1 red onion, chopped

1 package pepperoni

¼ cup black olives, optional

1 cup Italian dressing

½ cup parmesan cheese

Cook pasta and drain until cool. Chop vegetables. Mix all together in a bowl and stir. Sprinkle cheese on top. Chill overnight.

Serves: 8-10

Low-Fat Cole Slaw

1 bag of coleslaw

½ cup non-fat plain Greek yogurt (or light sour cream)

1-2 T. red cider vinegar

1 small can pineapple tidbits, drained

1/3 cup sunflower seeds

Mix yogurt, mayonnaise, and vinegar in a large bowl. Add coleslaw, pineapple, and toss. Chill several hours.

Serves: 4-6

Mango & Crouton Salad

1-2 mangoes

1 avocado

½ cup croutons

¼ cup Balsamic Vinegar

Slice mangoes and avocado. Place in a bowl. Toss with balsamic vinegar and sprinkle with croutons. Eat right away before the croutons become soggy!

Serves: 2

No-Lettuce Salad

2 to 3 tomatoes

2 avocados, sliced

1 red onion, chopped

1 cucumber peeled and sliced

1-2 T. olive oil

½-1 tsp. lemon juice

After slicing veggies and fruit, combine them in a bowl. Toss gently with oil and juice. Serves: 4

Mustard Potato Salad

A large bowl of leftover mashed potatoes

½ cup chopped onions

3 dill pickles, chopped

2 T. pickle juice

2-3 T. mustard

1-2 T. mayo (may use low-fat)

1-2 hard-boiled eggs, sliced (optional)

Set out leftover mashed potatoes until room temperature. (About thirty minutes.) Chop the onions and pickles. Add pickle juice, mustard, and mayo to the mashed potatoes and stir. Add the remaining ingredients and chill or eat immediately.

NOTE: While making a roast, I discovered I had too many leftover mashed potatoes. I called my mother and asked how to make mustard potato salad. She gave me this recipe which was also used by my late grandmother. It's a delicious way to use leftover mashed potatoes. By the way, the eggs are optional. I happened to be running low during the quarantine, so I left them out.

Pepper & Corn Salad

2 15 oz. cans corn, drained

6 green onions, chopped

1 green pepper, chopped

5 oz. green olives, drained and sliced

8 oz. Italian dressing

Drain the corn and add to a bowl. Chop veggies and olives. Stir into corn and add dressing. Eat immediately or chill and serve.

Serves: 6

Pineapple Cole Slaw

1 bag Cole slaw

½ red pepper, chopped

½ green pepper, chopped

½ red onion, chopped

1 8 oz. can pineapple tidbits, drained

1 cup fat-free mayo or plain Greek yogurt

Add Cole slaw to a large bowl. Chop peppers and onion. Add to slaw with pineapple and combine. Stir in mayo or yogurt. Chill. (My late father-in-law made this recipe, which we all enjoyed.)

Serves: 6-8

Taco Salad

1 pound ground beef

1 pkg. taco seasoning

1 8-oz. can tomato sauce

½ tsp. salt

¼ tsp. pepper

1 can red kidney beans, drained

1 small head lettuce, chopped

1 onion, chopped

½ cup grated cheddar cheese

Taco or corn chips

Brown hamburger and drain. Add taco seasoning and tomato sauce. Stir. Add beans to meat mixture and simmer on low heat for 10-15 minutes.

Add to a glass bowl. Top with lettuce, tomatoes, and onion. May layer or toss this salad. Before serving, add taco chips or corn chips.

Condiments that go well with this: salsa, guacamole and/or sour cream.

Serves: 4-6

Tomato Artichoke Salad

2 cans quartered artichoke hearts, drained

5-6 ripe tomatoes, cut in large wedges

1 green pepper, chopped

½ red onion, chopped

½ cup Zesty Italian salad dressing

Prepare vegetables and place in a bowl. Toss with salad dressing. Refrigerate for several hours or overnight. This salad is a summertime family favorite!

Serves 6-8

"Food is our common ground, a universal experience."
James Beard

Tomato & Red Onion Salad

4 tomatoes, thinly sliced

2 red onions, thinly sliced

2 T. red wine vinegar

1 T. olive oil

Arrange tomatoes and onions on a serving platter. Combine vinegar and olive oil. Drizzle over tomatoes and onions. Season to taste.

Serves: 4-6

"My weaknesses have always been food and men — in that order." Dolly Parton

Trees 'n Raisins Salad

One head broccoli, chopped

6-8 slices bacon, crumbled

½ cup raisins

½ cup red onion, chopped

1 cup mayo or plain Greek yogurt

¼-½ cup sugar or Splenda

2 T. white vinegar

½ cup peanuts or cashews, optional

Cook bacon and allow to cool. Chop vegetables.

Combine mayo/yogurt, sugar, and vinegar. Stir into vegetables. Add crumbled bacon and chill one hour. This has been a favorite for years!

Serves: 8

24-Hour Layered Salad

One head of lettuce, shredded or chopped

1 cup red onion, chopped

1 cup celery, diced

1 10-oz. can water chestnuts, drained and sliced

6 oz. pkg. frozen peas, thawed

2 cups Miracle Whip

1 tsp. sugar

¼ tsp. pepper

½ tsp. salt

½ cup parmesan cheese

1 cup cheddar cheese

5 slices bacon, optional

In a large glass bowl (so you can see the layers), place lettuce on the bottom. Add onions, celery, chestnuts, and peas. Spread Miracle Whip on top of peas. Mix sugar, pepper, and salt. Sprinkle on top of Miracle Whip. Add parmesan cheese and finally cheddar cheese. Cover and refrigerate overnight. Sprinkle with bacon before serving.

Serves: 10-12

Zucchini Mint Salad

4 zucchini, thinly sliced

¼ cup olive oil

2 T. lemon juice

1 T. fresh mint

¼ teaspoon salt

Two shakes of red or black pepper

In a large bowl, whisk the oil, lemon juice, salt, and pepper until blended. Add mint and zucchini. Mix well. Refrigerate until serving.

Serves: 4-6

"Let food be thy medicine and medicine be thy food."
Hippocrates

Side Dishes

Asparagus & Cherry Tomatoes

1-2 pounds asparagus

2 T. canola oil

½ tsp. salt

¼ tsp. pepper

1 pint cherry tomatoes, halved

2 tablespoons pesto, store-bought

Preheat oven to 375 degrees. On a cookie sheet or jelly roll pan, toss asparagus with oil. Sprinkle with salt and pepper. Roast asparagus until tender (approximately 15 minutes.) Stir halfway through cooking time.

In a separate bowl, toss cherry tomatoes with pesto. During last 5 minutes of cooking, add tomatoes to the asparagus and continue baking. This is a beautiful dish to serve around the holidays.

Serves 4

Asparagus & Pimientos

1 pound asparagus, trimmed

¼ cup bread crumbs

3 T. butter

2-3 T. grated parmesan cheese

2 T. chopped pimientos

In a saucepan over medium heat, cook asparagus in boiling water until crisp tender (7-8 minutes.) In a skillet, brown bread crumbs and butter. Drain asparagus and place on a serving dish. Sprinkle with bread crumbs, cheese, and pimentos.

This is an elegant side dish.

Serves: 4

Balsamic-Glazed Onions

1 T. Dijon mustard

1 T. balsamic vinegar

¼ cup honey

1 pound baby onions, halved

Combine mustard, vinegar, and honey in a medium saucepan. Bring to a boil. Simmer uncovered 5 minutes or until glaze thickens.

Cook onions in greased, heated skillet. Toss several times, then brush constantly with balsamic glaze. Stir often until browned.

Serves: 6

Basil Cherry Tomatoes

2 pints cherry tomatoes

2 T. fresh or dried basil

¼ cup olive or canola oil

Salt and pepper to taste

Toss cherry tomatoes with oil. Add basil, salt and pepper. Serve immediately or refrigerate. Simple and easy. (Using fresh basil is by far the tastiest way to make this if you have it on hand.)

Serves: 4-6

Beanie Beanie Casserole

Layer in order:

> 2 cans pork and beans
>
> 1 onion, sliced
>
> 4 potatoes, peeled and sliced thinly
>
> 8-10 slices of uncooked bacon
>
> 2 cans green beans, drained
>
> 4-6 tomatoes, sliced
>
> ½ cup parmesan cheese
>
> Salt & pepper to taste
>
> Butter

Preheat oven to 375 degrees. Beginning with the beans, layer all in a 9 by 13 pan. After each layer, sprinkle salt and pepper and a few dots of butter, if desired. Add parmesan cheese to the top, cover, and bake for 45 minutes. Uncover and cook 15 minutes longer. This is unique, plus it uses several pantry items.

Serves: 10-12

Beth's Famous Baked Beans

4 cans pork and beans

¾ cup onion, chopped

½ cup green pepper, chopped

1 T. Worcestershire sauce

1 tsp. mustard

½ cup ketchup

1 T. brown sugar (may use Splenda)

4 slices bacon, cooked and torn into one-inch pieces

After prepping vegetables, stir beans into a bowl. Add onion, green pepper, Worcestershire sauce, mustard, ketchup, and sugar. Top with bacon. Bake uncovered at 325 degrees for one hour.

Serves: 8-10

"When the waitress asked if I wanted my pizza cut into four or eight slices, I said, 'Four. I don't think I can eat eight.'" Yogi Berra

Broccoli & Rice Casserole

1 box frozen broccoli, cooked

1 ½ cups rice, cooked

1 can cream of mushroom soup

8 oz. Cheese Whiz

½ cup celery, chopped

½ cup onion, chopped

1 T. butter

Sauté onion and celery in a skillet with butter. Microwave broccoli according to package instructions. Cook rice according to the package. Combine all ingredients while hot which helps to melt the cheese. Stir well and place in a greased casserole dish. Bake for 30 minutes at 350 degrees. Even though this uses several pans, it's totally worth the effort and is a must-have casserole at every family gathering.

Serves: 10 (unless my brother is there!)

Broccoli & Sour Cream Casserole

2 16-oz. packages frozen broccoli florets

1 can cream of mushroom soup

1 cup sour cream

1 ½ cups shredded cheddar cheese, divided

1 6 oz. can French fried onions, divided.

Cook broccoli according to package directions and drain. In a large sauce pan, combine the soup, sour cream, 1 cup cheddar cheese, and three-fourths of the French fried onions. Cook over medium heat for 4-5 minutes. Add the broccoli and stir well.

Pour into a greased 9 x 13 baking dish. Bake uncovered at 325 degrees for 25 minutes. Sprinkle with remaining cheese and onions. Bake 10 minutes longer.

Serves: 8

Broccolini & Honey

1-2 pounds broccolini, halved horizontally

1 T. soy sauce

2 tsp. honey

2 tsp. sesame seeds, toasted

Cook broccolini in large saucepan in simmering water for five minutes or until fork tender. Combine soy sauce and honey. Place broccolini in a serving dish. Drizzle with sauce and sprinkle with toasted sesame seeds.

Serves: 4

Brussels Sprouts with Cranberries

1 pound Brussels sprouts, halved

½ cup olive oil

Salt and pepper to taste

½ cup dried cranberries

Preheat oven to 400 degrees. Wash and halve Brussels sprouts. Place in a jelly roll pan. Drizzle with oil, salt and pepper, and toss.

Bake 15-18 minutes. Add cranberries. Bake another 5 minutes or until Brussels sprouts are crisp-tender.

Serves: 4

"If you can't feed a hundred people, then feed just one."
Mother Teresa

Candied Carrots

1 package small carrots

1/3 cup orange juice

¼ cup Maple syrup (may use sugar-free)

5 T. butter

½ tsp. nutmeg

¼ cup fresh parsley (or 1 tsp. dried)

Combine all ingredients (except parsley) in a saucepan. Stir well. Cover and simmer for 20 minutes until carrots are fork tender. Garnish with parsley.

Serves: 4

Creamy Dill Cucumbers

1 cup regular (or skim milk)

½ cup mayo

½ cup sour cream (low-fat is optional)

1 envelope Ranch salad dressing mix

2 T. dill

1/8 tsp. celery seed

1/8 tsp. pepper

3 large cucumbers, peeled and sliced

2/3 cup red onion, chopped

Combine milk, mayo, sour cream, dressing, dill, celery seed, and pepper. Stir in cucumbers and onions. Mix well. Serve with a slotted spoon.

Serves: 6-8

Drunken Cranberries

2 bags fresh cranberries

1 ½ cups sugar or Splenda

¼ cup Brandy

1 orange

Stir cranberries, sugar, and brandy together in a large bowl. Grate orange into a smaller bowl. Add the orange zest, plus a couple of squirts of the juice. Combine well and place in a 9 x 13 dish.

Bake at 300 degrees for 40 minutes. This is a simple, fast way to prepare cranberries over the holidays.

Serves: 8-10

"Once you get a spice in your home, you have it forever. Women never throw out spices. The Egyptians were buried with their spices. I know which one I'm taking with me when I go." Erma Bombeck

Fiesta Corn

8 oz. cream cheese (fat-free is fine)

4 cans whole kernel corn, drained

1-2 cans chopped green chilies

6 green onions, chopped

1 red pepper, chopped

In a large sauce pan, heat the cream cheese until softened. Add the corn, green chilies, green onions, and red pepper. Stir well. Cook until heated through and serve.

NOTE: This dish may be kept warm in a crock pot for several hours. We often serve this with a variety of entrees.

Serves: 8-10

Grandma's Green Beans

4 cans green bens

7 strips bacon

1/3 stick butter

Salt & pepper to taste

Add all ingredients to a large sauce pan. Cook on medium high for one or two hours. Add extra water as it cooks down. This isn't the healthiest way to eat green beans but our family sure loved them when Grandma made this dish!

Serves: 6

"If this is coffee, please bring me some tea; but if this is tea, please bring me some coffee." Abraham Lincoln

Microwave Greek Green Beans

2 pounds fresh green beans, cut into 2 inch pieces

2 T. olive oil

2 tablespoons fresh garlic, minced

½ tsp. salt

¾ cup herbed feta cheese

In a microwave-safe dish combine the beans, oil, garlic, and salt. Microwave on high for 5 to 7 minutes. Stir occasionally. Top with feta cheese.

Serves: 4

Mint Peas

1 pound frozen peas

2 cloves garlic, unpeeled

½ cup plain yogurt

½ cup fresh mint

Boil water. Carefully, add peas and garlic. Cook until peas are softened. Drain water. After it's cooled, peel garlic and add yogurt, peas, and mint. Stir until blended.

Serves: 4

Onion Potatoes

8 medium russet potatoes, chopped in large chunks

2 envelopes Lipton dry onion soup

¾ cup olive oil

Preheat oven to 425. Combine all ingredients in a large bowl and transfer to a 9 by 13 ungreased baking dish. Bake 35 to 40 minutes. NOTE: After cooking, the potatoes may be kept warm for hours in a crock pot using the low setting.

We love this three-ingredient recipe. The potatoes go well with chicken or pork. We discovered this delicious recipe on the Lipton dry onion soup packet.

Serves: 12

"I have made a lot of mistakes falling in love, and regretted most of them, but never the potatoes that went with them." Nora Ephron

Parmesan Potatoes

8 russet potatoes, unpeeled

3 T. grated parmesan cheese

6 T. butter

Preheat oven to 400 degrees. Place butter slices in a 9 x 13-inch baking pan. Put in oven for five minutes or until butter is melted. Remove from the oven and sprinkle the parmesan cheese over the melted butter. Arrange potatoes cut side down over the cheese. Bake uncovered 40-45 minutes. Serve right side up on a platter—they're prettier that way.

Using only three ingredients, these potatoes have been a favorite for decades. They're delicious with almost any entrée and are often requested on holidays or birthdays.

Serves: 8

Parmesan Noodles

1 8 oz. package egg noodles (or bow tie pasta),
uncooked

1 stick butter

¾ cup parmesan cheese

½ tsp. salt

¼ tsp. pepper

½ T. parsley (for garnish)

Cook noodles according to package directions. Drain. In a large saucepan, melt the better and remaining ingredients (except parsley). When thoroughly blended and butter is melted, add hot noodles. Stir until coated. Top with parsley and serve immediately.

Serves: 4-6

"The most remarkable thing about my mother is that for 30 years she served the family nothing but leftovers. The original meal has never been found." Calvin Trillin

Roasted Asparagus

1 lb. asparagus

1 T. olive oil

2-3 T. parmesan cheese

Salt and pepper to taste

Balsamic vinegar

Preheat oven to 425 degrees. Place asparagus in single layer on a pan with edges. Drizzle with olive oil, salt, pepper and toss. Add parmesan cheese.

Bake for 13 to 15 minutes. In a separate serving dish, drizzle balsamic vinegar on the bottom of the plate. Transfer hot asparagus to dish and enjoy.

NOTE: The balsamic vinegar is optional. This is just as good without it.

Roasted Broccoli

Same recipe as above, minus the balsamic vinegar. Easy and delicious! You may also omit the parmesan cheese.

Roasted Cauliflower

Guess what? Same recipe as Roasted Asparagus and Roasted Broccoli.

Ruby Red Pears

1 29-oz. can pear halves, drained

1 16-oz. can whole berry cranberry sauce

¼ cup sugar (or Splenda)

2 T. lemon juice

¼ tsp. cinnamon

Preheat oven to 350 degrees. Place pairs cut side up in a greased 8-inch square baking dish. In a saucepan, combine cranberry sauce, sugar, lemon juice, and cinnamon. Cook and stir until sugar is dissolved. After heating through, spoon mixture into the pear indentions.

Bake uncovered for 25-30 minutes. This is a beautiful recipe.

Serves: 4-6

"If we're not supposed to have midnight snacks, then why is there a light in the fridge?" Author unknown

Sesame Broccoli Spears

10 oz. frozen broccoli spears (or florets)

1 T. vegetable or canola oil

1 T. soy sauce

1 T. sugar (or Splenda)

2 tsp. white vinegar

2 tsp. sesame seeds, toasted

Cook broccoli on the stove or in the microwave according to package directions. In a small saucepan combine oil, soy sauce, sugar, and vinegar. Heat on medium until sugar is dissolved. Toast sesame seeds in a skillet on medium heat for 1-2 minutes. It doesn't take long.

Drain broccoli and place in a serving dish. Top with soy sauce mixture and sprinkle with sesame seeds.

Steamed Asparagus

1 pound asparagus

Dash salt

½ tsp. lemon pepper

Cut thick ends off asparagus. Use 5-6" stems so they'll fit into a medium-sized saucepan. Place in a double boiler. Sprinkle with salt and lemon pepper. Cover and heat on medium for 5-7 minutes until crisp tender.

Serves: 2

Steamed Broccoli

1 pound broccoli

Dash salt

½ tsp. lemon pepper

Cut long stems off broccoli and cut into florets. Place in a double boiler. Sprinkle with salt and lemon pepper. Cover and heat on medium for 5-7 minutes until crisp tender.

Serves: 2

Speedy Microwave Sweet Potatoes

2 16-oz. cans sweet potatoes, drained

½ tsp. salt

1 8-oz. can crushed pineapple, drained

¼ cup chopped pecans

1 T. brown sugar (May use Splenda)

1 cup miniature marshmallows, divided

½ tsp. ground nutmeg

In a 1 ½ quart microwave safe dish, layer sweet potatoes, salt, pineapple, pecans, brown sugar, and half a cup of marshmallows. Cover and microwave on high 5-7 minutes or until bubbly. Top with remaining marshmallows and heat uncovered another 1-2 minutes. Sprinkle with nutmeg.

This is the perfect holiday dish since it's made in the microwave and frees up oven space. I always double it to feed our family.

Serves: 4

Sweet Potato Casserole

3 small cans or 2 large cans sweet potatoes, drained

¾ cup sugar

1 cup evaporated milk

3/4 stick butter

3 beaten eggs

Preheat oven to 400 degrees. Drain and mash sweet potatoes in a large mixing bowl. Add remaining ingredients and blend. Place in 9 by 13 baking dish. Bake at 400 degrees for 20-25 minutes.

Topping:

> 1/3 cup sugar or Splenda
>
> 1 stick butter, melted
>
> 2 cups Corn Flakes, crushed
>
> 1 cup coconut
>
> ½ cup chopped pecans

While the casserole bakes, melt butter in the microwave and crush the cornflakes on a plate. Mix all ingredients in a bowl. When the casserole is out of the oven, spread the mixture on top. Bake at 400 degrees for 8-10 minutes. This is another must-have family favorite. Serves: 10

Sweet Potato Fries

2 medium sweet potatoes, peeled

2 T. olive oil

1 T. brown sugar (or Splenda)

½ tsp. sea salt

¼ tsp. black pepper

Preheat oven to 450 degrees. Slice sweet potatoes lengthwise into long spears. Place on baking sheet and toss with olive oil. Combine brown sugar, salt, and pepper. Sprinkle on potatoes. Bake 15 minutes. Toss with spatula and bake another 5 minutes or until brown. Sprinkle with additional salt or pepper as desired.

Baked fries are definitely healthier and still delicious. If you try this with regular potatoes, leave off the brown sugar and add parmesan cheese and parsley!

Serves: 4

Traditional Green Bean Casserole

4 cans green beans, drained

1 can Golden Mushroom soup

1 can French fried onion rings

Salt & Pepper to taste

Preheat oven to 350 degrees. Place drained green beans on the bottom of a 9 x 13 dish or large oven-proof bowl. Top with a layer of Golden Mushroom soup. Add salt and pepper to taste. Add three-fourths of the French fried onion rings and bake for 20 minutes.

Remove from oven. Top with remaining onion rings and bake another 3-5 minutes or until golden brown. This recipe has been in most people's homes—in some variation—for decades, I'm sure. We prefer using the Golden Mushroom soup but many use traditional cream of mushroom soup. Use whichever one is in your pantry!

Serves: 6-8

Soups

Black Bean Soup

Four cans black bean soup

2 cans Rotel tomatoes (or 1 jar chunky salsa)

1 medium onion, chopped

1 green pepper, chopped

2 T. minced garlic

1 can vegetable broth

1 tsp. salt

½ tsp. pepper

Mix beans, tomatoes/salsa, onion, pepper, garlic, broth, and seasonings in a large bowl. Transfer to a slow cooker. Cook on low for 6-7 hours.

If desired mash some of the beans for a thicker consistency. Serve over rice or with cornbread.

Serves: 6

Broccoli Cheese Soup

2 T. butter or margarine

5 cups water

8 oz. fine egg noodles

1/4 tsp. garlic powder

½ pound American cheese or Velveeta, grated or chopped

3/4 cup onion, chopped

6 chicken bouillon cubes

2 10-oz. packages frozen broccoli, thawed

6 cups milk

Lemon pepper seasoning to taste

Sauté onion in butter. Add water and bouillon cubes, bring to a boil. Gradually add noodles and cook uncovered three minutes. Stir in broccoli and garlic. Cook another four minutes. Add milk and cheese. Stir until cheese melts but do not boil.

Serves: 10-12

"Only the pure in heart can make a good soup."
Beethoven

Canned Vegetable Soup

1 large can potatoes and green beans, drained

1 can Fiesta corn, drained

1 can sliced carrots, drained

1 can zucchini with Italian tomato sauce

1 can diced tomatoes with basil, garlic, and oregano

1 can chicken or beef broth

1 tsp. dry minced onion

½ tsp. lemon pepper seasoning

1 tsp. parsley

¼-½ tsp. pepper

1 Bay leaf

Drain the first 3 cans of soup and combine all ingredients in a large pot. Add remaining spices and stir. Bring to a boil and reduce heat. Simmer 10-15 minutes. Keep warm until served. Discard bay leaf before serving.

This is surprisingly delicious, and best of all, no chopping is required! Use whatever cans of vegetables you have in your pantry.

Serves: 6 to 8

Chili

1 lb. hamburger

½ cup onion, chopped

½ - ¾ packet of chili seasoning

2 cans red kidney beans or chili beans

1 can diced or stewed tomatoes

1 small can tomato sauce

1 can chopped green chilies, optional

1 small can corn, drained (optional)

1 can lima beans, drained (optional)

Sauté onion and hamburger in a large stock pan until browned. Drain grease. Add beans, tomatoes, tomato sauce, chili powder, and any other optional canned vegetables listed above. Cook over medium heat 20 minutes until thickens. Simmer on low for another 10 minutes.

Make your chili your own. I sometimes add chopped green pepper or one-third a cup of red wine vinegar. Experiment with a variety of ingredients and have fun with it.

Serves: 4

Curried Pumpkin Soup

1 small onion, chopped

1 tsp. canola oil

1 can of pumpkin

1 tsp. lemon juice

1 tsp. curry powder

1 can low-sodium chicken broth

1 tsp. sugar or Splenda

½ tsp. seasoning blend

Dash pepper

Parsley (to taste)

½ cup evaporated skim milk

In a sauce pan over medium heat, sauté the onion until tender. Add chicken broth, pumpkin, spices (except parsley), and lemon juice. Bring to boil. Reduce heat. Cover and simmer for 15 minutes. Stir in skim milk and heat through. Garnish with parsley. Serves: 4

"Anyone who's a chef, who loves food, ultimately knows that all that matters is: 'Is it good? Does it give pleasure?'" Anthony Bourdain

Easy Cheese Broccoli Soup

1 head broccoli, chopped (or use frozen broccoli, thawed)

2 cans cream of mushroom or cream of chicken soup

1 cup milk

8-16 oz. cheddar cheese, grated

1 tsp. Worcestershire sauce

½ tsp. lemon pepper seasoning

¼ tsp. paprika

½ tsp. salt

Combine all ingredients in a slow cooker. Cover and cook on low 4-6 hours. Stir thoroughly before serving.

Serves: 4

"I come from a family where gravy is considered a beverage." Erma Bombeck

Onion Soup

3 medium onions, thinly sliced

¼ cup butter

1 tsp. salt

½ tsp. pepper

1 T. sugar or Splenda

2 T. flour

2 cans beef or vegetable broth

½ cup dry white wine

Swiss or parmesan cheese

After slicing onions, add butter to skillet. Sauté onions while covered until soft. Add salt, pepper, and sugar. Cook uncovered another 15 minutes. Stir in flour and cook 3 more minutes. Add onions, broth, and wine to a slow cooker and cook on low 6-7 hours.

Before serving, sprinkle with grated cheese, if desired. Serve with French, sourdough or garlic bread.

Serves: 6

Potato Soup

8 russet potatoes, peeled and cubed

1 onion, chopped

1 carrot, chopped (I prefer a handful of shredded carrots)

2 ribs of celery, diced

4 chicken or vegetable bouillon cubes

1 T. parsley flakes

4-5 cups water

½ tsp. pepper

1 T. sea salt

1/3 cup butter, melted

½ package dry potato soup mix (optional but helps thicken)

1 tsp. lemon pepper seasoning

12 oz. can evaporated milk (use later)

2 cups milk (add much later!)

After chopping and dicing vegetables, combine all ingredients (except milk) in a large crockpot. Cook on low 7-8 hours. Stir in evaporated milk last hour of cooking time. Add regular, fresh or skim milk last 15 minutes of cooking time.

Serves: 8-10 (freezes well)

Sausage & Kale Soup

2 cans chicken broth

½ cup heavy cream

3 carrots, grated

4 potatoes peeled and cubed

4 cups kale, chopped

1 pound spicy Italian sausage, browned

1 tsp. salt

½ tsp. crushed red pepper flakes

Combine broth and cream in slow cooker. Add carrots, potatoes, kale, and sausage. Sprinkle spices over top. Sir well.

Cook on high 4-5 hours, stirring occasionally.

Serves: 4

Southwestern Bean Soup

1 can black bean soup or black beans

2 15 oz. cans red kidney beans, drained

2 15 oz. cans navy or pinto beans, drained

1 16 oz. jar chunky salsa, mild or medium

1 4.5 oz. can chopped green chilies

½ cup red wine vinegar

Spray a slow cooker with cooking spray. In a mixing bowl, add the beans, red wine vinegar, and salsa. Mix well. Transfer to the crock pot. Cover and cook on low for 6-7 hours. This soup makes a generous amount and freezes well.

This is my all-time favorite soup for fall and winter! Actually, I eat it year round. Feel free to vary the type of beans and use whatever you have in your pantry.

Serves 8-10

Serve with cornbread or salad.

"The belly rules the mind."

Spanish Proverb

Taco Soup

1 pound ground beef

1 onion, chopped

16 oz. can Mexican-style stewed or diced tomatoes

2 16 oz. can red kidney beans, undrained

16 oz. can corn, drained

16 oz. can black beans, undrained

16 oz. jar picante sauce

1 4.5 oz. can chopped green chiles, undrained

Tortilla chips

Sour cream

Shredded cheddar cheese

Brown ground beef and onion in skillet until meat is no longer pink. Drain. Combine tomatoes, corn, beans, picante sauce, and chiles in slow cooker. Add meat and onions. Stir well. Cook on low 6-8 hours.

Serve with tortilla chips, sour cream, or cheddar cheese.

Serves: 6-8

Vegetable Beef Soup

1 pound stew meat (optional if you prefer vegetarian)

1 1-lb can of tomatoes

5-6 carrots, sliced

2 stalks celery with tops, chopped

1 medium onion, diced

4-5 potatoes, diced

3-4 cups water

1 tsp. salt

4 beef bouillon cubes

1 16 oz. pkg. frozen mixed vegetables

1 bay leaf

8-10 peppercorns

2 T. parsley flakes

½ T. lemon pepper

10 oz. can tomato juice (optional)

Place all ingredients in a crockpot and stir well. Cover and cook on low for 10-12 hours (or on high for 6 hours.) This was my daughter's favorite soup as a child!

Serves: 8-10

Entrees

Artichoke chicken

1 14 oz. can water packed quartered artichoke hearts, well drained and chopped

¾ cup grated parmesan cheese

¾ cup mayonnaise (do not use fat free or light Mayo)

Dash garlic powder

Paprika

4 boneless, skinless chicken breasts

Combine the artichokes, cheese, mayo and garlic powder in a bowl. Place chicken in a greased 7 x 11 baking dish. Spread artichoke mixture on top. Sprinkle with paprika.

Bake uncovered at 375 degrees for 30 to 35 minutes. This is my husband's favorite chicken recipe!

Serves: 2-4

"Wine is bottled poetry." Robert Louis Stevenson

Asian Salmon

4 Salmon filets

1/3 cup honey

1/3 cup green onion, chopped

2 T. soy sauce

2 tsp. sesame seeds, toasted

1 tsp. minced garlic

1 tsp. minced onions

¾ tsp. ground ginger

1/2 tsp. crushed red pepper

Preheat oven to 375 degrees. Mix honey, green onion, and soy sauce. Add all spices except red pepper. Stir until blended. Add red pepper to taste.

Place salmon in a 9 x 13 baking dish. Spray lightly with lemon oil. Spoon honey mixture on top. Bake for 20 minutes or until fish flakes.

Serves: 2-4

"I'm on a seafood diet. I see food and I eat it."
Anonymous

Bacon Asparagus Quiche

1 deep-dish unbaked pastry shell

1 lb. fresh asparagus, cooked and cut into 1-inch pieces

6 bacon strips, cooked

3 eggs

1 ¼ cups half and half

2-3 sliced green onions, including tops

¾ cup grated parmesan cheese, divided

1 tsp. sugar or Splenda

½ tsp. salt

¼ tsp. pepper

2 shakes of ground nutmeg

Preheat oven to 450 degrees. Line pastry shell with 2 sheets of aluminum foil. Bake for 5 minutes. Remove foil and bake 5 minutes longer. Remove pie shell from oven and let cool. Cook asparagus in a small amount of water until crisp tender, about 3 minutes. Drain and allow to cool. In the microwave or a skillet, cook bacon until crisp. When cool, tear into bite-sized pieces.

In a bowl, add eggs, cream, ½ cup cheese, onions, seasonings. Arrange bacon and asparagus in the pie shell. Top with the cheese mixture. Sprinkle with remaining cheese. Bake at 400 for 10 minutes. Reduce heat to 350 degrees and bake an additional 35-40 minutes. Serves: 6-8

Barbecue Beef & Biscuits

¾ pound ground beef

½ c barbecue sauce

1 T. instant minced onion

1 can flaky biscuits

¾ c shredded cheddar cheese

Preheat oven to 400 degrees. Brown hamburger and drain. Add barbecue sauce and onion to the skillet and stir until heated through.

Separate biscuit dough and place each biscuit in an ungreased muffin tin, pressing dough on the bottom and up the sides. Spoon meat mixture into biscuit cups and bake 10 to 15 minutes. Sprinkle with cheddar cheese. The kids and grands will enjoy this dish.

Yield: 10 to 12 muffins

Barbecue Pork Chops

4 pork loin chops, three quarter inch thick, trim the fat.

1 cup ketchup

1 cup hot water

2 T. white vinegar

1 tablespoon Worcestershire sauce

2 teaspoons brown sugar

1/2 tsp. black pepper

1/2 tsp. chili powder

1/2 tsp. paprika

Place pork chops in a slow cooker. Combine remaining ingredients and pour over the chops. Cover and cook on high 5-6 hours.

Serves: 4

"Eat breakfast like a king, lunch like a prince, and dinner like a pauper." Adelle Davis

Barbecue Ribs

3-4 lbs. pork ribs (boneless or bone-in)

1/4 cup balsamic vinegar

2 T. Worcestershire sauce

2 T. Dijon mustard

½ a bottle of your favorite barbecue sauce

2 T. maple syrup (may use sugar free)

2 tsp. hot sauce

¾ cup white vinegar

½ cup catsup

1 tsp. paprika

½ tsp. ground mustard

1-2 garlic cloves

½ tsp. salt

¼ tsp. pepper

Place ribs in slow cooker. Mix remaining ingredients. Pour over ribs and cook on low 8 hours.

NOTE: May use the same delicious sauce for pork chops!

Serves: 6-8

Black Bean Pie

½ pound ground beef

½ cup onion, chopped

½ cup green pepper, chopped

1 15-oz. can black beans, rinsed and drained

1 cup salsa

1 8 ½ oz. package cornbread mix

¼ cup milk

1 egg

2 cups shredded cheddar cheese, divided

Sour cream, guacamole, and additional salsa, optional

Preheat oven to 375 degrees. Brown ground beef, onion, and green pepper in a skillet until meat is no longer pink. Drain. Stir in black beans and salsa.

In a separate bowl, combine muffin mix, milk, eggs, and one cup of cheddar cheese. Pour cornbread mixture into a greased 9 inch pie plate. Bake for 5 minutes. Remove from oven and add meat mixture, leaving a ½ inch edge. Bake another 15-18 minutes until golden brown. Sprinkle with cheese and bake 1-2 minutes longer until cheese is melted. Serve with sour cream, guacamole, and/or salsa as desired.

Serves: 6-8

Cajun Cod

4 cod filets (or other white fish)

2 T. Cajun seasoning

2 teaspoons lemon zest

1 T. canola oil

Preheat oven to 425 degrees. Combine seasoning, lemon zest, and oil in small bowl. Mix well and rub over fish.

Bake fish for 12-15 minutes until cooked through and flakes easily with a fork.

Serves: 4

Cashew Chicken Casserole

4 cups cubed, cooked chicken

2 T. butter

1 cup celery, chopped

½ cup onion, chopped (I prefer using green onions)

2 cans cream of mushroom soup (or cream of chicken)

2 cups cooked rice

2 cups chicken broth

6-8 T. soy sauce

2 ½ cups cashews

1 small can Chinese noodles

Preheat oven to 350 degrees. Sauté onion and celery in butter. Mix all ingredients, except noodles and cashews, in a bowl. Stir well and pour into a 9 by 13 pan. Bake for 30 minutes. Top with noodles and cashews. Bake another five minutes or until browned.

Serves: 8-10

Cheeseburger & Fries Casserole

1-2 pounds ground beef

1 can golden mushroom soup

1 can cheddar cheese soup

1 20-oz. pkg. frozen crinkle cut fries (or tater tots)

Preheat oven to 350 degrees. In a skillet, brown the ground beef until no longer pink. Drain. Stir in the soups. Pour mixture into a greased 9 by 13 baking dish.

Arrange French fries or tater tots on top and bake uncovered for 50-55 minutes until the fries are golden brown. This likely isn't the healthiest meal, but it'll put a smile on kids' faces (and yours!) Feel free to serve with a green salad.

Serves: 10-12

Creamy Herbed Chicken

4 boneless chicken breasts

1 can condensed cream of chicken or mushroom soup

1 cup milk

One envelope Knorr's garlic and herb pasta sauce mix

1 tsp. dried thyme

1 tsp. dried parsley flakes

Salt and pepper to taste

Cooked noodles or rice

Place chicken in a slow cooker. Salt and pepper to taste. Combine the soup, milk, sauce mix, and seasonings in a bowl. Pour over the chicken.

Cook on low five or six hours or until juices run clear. Serve over hot noodles or rice. The sauce makes a great gravy.

"Cooking is like love. It should be entered into with abandon or not at all." Julia Child

Crispy Almost-Fried Chicken

4 cups Rice Krispies cereal (I've also used Corn Flakes or sour cream and green onion potato chips!)

¾ cup parmesan cheese, grated

2 T. olive oil

1 tsp. paprika

1 tsp. salt

1 tsp. oregano

1 tsp. pepper

1 tsp. garlic

1 cup low-fat plain yogurt or melted butter

8 boneless skinless chicken breasts

Preheat oven to 350 degrees. Line baking sheet with foil. Combine rice cereal, parmesan, oil, and seasonings. Brush both sides of the chicken with yogurt (or dip in melted butter.)

Coat with cereal mixture. Bake 30-35 minutes until golden brown.

Serves: 2-4

"The best comfort food will always be greens, cornbread, and fried chicken." Maya Angelou

Crock Pot BBQ Chicken

4 skinless chicken breasts

1 can condensed tomato soup

¾ cup onion, chopped

¼ cup white or red wine vinegar

½ T. brown sugar (may use Splenda)

1 T. Worcestershire sauce

½ tsp. salt

¼ tsp. dried basil

¼ tsp. thyme

1/3 to 1/2 cup green peppers, chopped

Place meat in a slow cooker. Add green pepper, if desired. Combine all other ingredients and pour over chicken or pork. Cover and cook on low 6-8 hours.

Serves: 4

Crock Pot Pork Chops

4 pork chops

¼ cup extra virgin olive oil

1 can chicken broth

2-3 garlic cloves, minced

1 tsp. dried basil

1 tsp. oregano

½ tsp. Italian seasoning

Salt & Pepper (to taste)

Rinse off pork chops and place in a slow cooker. Salt and pepper to taste. Mix remaining ingredients and pour over pork chops. Cook on low for 5-7 hours.

Serves: 4

Crunchy Onion Chicken

1 1/3 cups French Fried Onions

4 skinless chicken breasts

1 egg beaten

¼ tsp. garlic powder

¼ tsp. paprika

¼ tsp. thyme

2-3 T. parmesan cheese

Preheat oven to 400 degrees. Crush French fried onions in plastic bag. Stir in spices and cheese. Dip chicken in egg; coat with onion crumbs. Place on a baking sheet and bake 20 minutes or until cooked through.

"He was a bold man that first ate an oyster." Jonathan Swift

French Dip Sandwiches

½ roast, shredded (using leftover roast!)

2 cups water

½ cup soy sauce (lite is fine)

1 tsp. dried rosemary

1 tsp. garlic powder (or fresh minced garlic)

1 tsp. dried thyme

1 Bay leaf

Few peppercorns (optional)

Wheat rolls

This is absolutely the best way to use leftover roast! Preheat oven to 350 degrees. Place shredded meat in a 9" square baking dish. Mix water, soy sauce, and seasonings. Pour over the roast.

Cover with foil and reheat in oven for 20-25 minutes. Using a slotted spoon, separate beef from au jus (juice). Place juice in separate ramekins for dunking. Place meat on bottom halves of the wheat rolls. Top with bread, cut on the diagonal (because it's prettier) and serve with sweet potato fries. Delicious!

Serves: 4-6

Frito Chili Casserole

3 cups corn chips

1 large onion, chopped

2 ½ cups chili (19 oz. can)

1 cup grated cheddar cheese

Preheat oven to 350 degrees. Place half the corn chips in a baking dish. Sprinkle with the onions and half of the cheese. Top with chili and remaining corn chips and cheese. Bake for 15 to 20 minutes. Easy peasy when you're in a rush or tired.

Serves: 6

Garlicky Chicken

4 boneless, skinless chicken breasts

4-6 cloves garlic, chopped

¼ cup olive oil

½ cup parmesan cheese

½ cup seasoned bread crumbs

Preheat oven to 425 degrees. Chop garlic and add to a bowl with olive oil. Place in a microwave safe dish large enough to hold a chicken breast. Microwave on high for three minutes and set aside.

In another bowl, combine parmesan cheese and bread crumbs. Dip chicken in garlic oil and then coat with bread crumb mixture.

Place in an ungreased 9 x 13 pan. Bake for 30 to 35 minutes or until juices are clear. I think this recipe would also work well with fish. Just don't bake it quite as long.

Serves: 4

Goulash

1 pound hamburger

1 2 lb. jar original spaghetti sauce (Ragu, Prego, etc.)

1/2 onion, chopped

1/2 tsp. garlic salt

1/2 bag shell macaroni

1 cup sharp cheddar cheese, shredded

1 cup parmesan cheese

Preheat oven to 350 degrees. Brown hamburger and onion until no longer pink. Drain. Meanwhile, boil macaroni and milk together and simmer for a few minutes. Pour into a 9 by 13 inch pan. Sprinkle top with cheddar cheese followed by parmesan cheese.

Bake for 25 minutes.

Serves: 6-8

Gourmet Hot Dogs

¾ cup onion, chopped

3 T. butter

1 ½ cups celery, chopped

1 ½ cups catchup

¾ cup water

1/3 cup lemon juice

3 T. brown sugar

3 T. white vinegar

1 T. Worcestershire sauce

1 T. yellow mustard

2 packages all-beef hot dogs

20 hot dog buns

Preheat oven to 350 degrees. In a saucepan over medium heat, sauté onion in butter until tender. Add remaining ingredients except hot dogs and buns. Bring to a boil. Reduce heat and cover. Simmer for 30 minutes. Cut three ¼-inch slits in hot dogs. Place in a baking dish. Pour the sauce over the hot dogs. Cover and bake for 40 minutes. Serve on buns.

I once took these to a pool party and they were a big hit!

Serves: 20

Hamburger Biscuit Casserole

1 pound ground beef

½ cup onion, chopped

1 cup barbecue sauce

1 T. brown sugar (may use Splenda)

1 16-oz. can baked beans

1 10-oz. can flaky or buttermilk biscuits

½ cup shredded cheddar cheese

Preheat oven to 375 degrees. In a large skillet, brown ground beef and onion until no longer pink. Drain grease.

Add barbecue sauce, brown sugar, and beans to meat mixture. Heat until bubbly.

Pour into a 2 ½ quart round casserole dish. Separate biscuits and cut each one in half lengthwise. Place biscuits along the edges on top of the meat mixture. Sprinkle cheese over the biscuits.

Big 20-25 minutes or until biscuits are golden brown.

I made this dish when I was first married and barely knew how to cook. I served it to company once with fresh cucumbers and cantaloupe and they thought it was grand.

Serves: 6

Kraut & Chops

2 cups barbecue sauce

1 cup water

4 lean pork chops

1-2 lbs. sauerkraut

Combine barbecue sauce and water in a small bowl. Place sauerkraut and pork chops in the bottom of a slow cooker. Pour sauce over the top.

Cover and cook on low setting for 8 hours.

Serves: 4

Parmesan Chicken

4-6 chicken breasts

¾ cup dry bread crumbs

1/3 cup grated parmesan cheese

¼ cup almonds, sliced or slivered (optional but good!)

2 T. dried parsley

1 tsp. salt

¼ tsp. pepper

¼ tsp. ground thyme

1 stick butter, melted

1 tsp. garlic powder

Preheat oven to 350 degrees. Combine crumbs, cheese, almonds, parsley, salt, pepper, pepper, and thyme in a mixing bowl. Meanwhile place butter in a 9 x 13 baking dish for 2-3 minutes until butter is melted. Sprinkle with garlic.

Dip chicken in butter and then in crumb mixture. Place in baking dish. Cook uncovered for 45-50 minutes. Do not turn chicken. Cover with foil if it's getting too brown toward the end. This is a family-favorite, often requested dish!

Serves: 4-6

Pecan-Crusted Salmon

2-4 salmon filets

1-2 T. mayonnaise

½ cup finely chopped pecans or almonds

1/3 cup seasoned bread crumbs

3 ½ T. grated parmesan cheese

1 T. fresh parsley

½ T. garlic salt

1 tablespoon butter, melted

Preheat oven to 425 degrees. Place salmon skin side down in a greased 7 x 11 baking dish. Spread 1 tablespoon mayonnaise over each filet. Combine the pecans, bread crumbs, parmesan cheese, parsley and butter; Spoon over salmon.

Bake for 10 to 15 minutes or until fish flakes easily with a fork.

Serves: 2-4

Pork Roast

1 can Coca-Cola

1 cup barbecue sauce

2-3 garlic cloves, chopped

3 scallions, chopped

Rinse and place pork in a slow cooker. Mix remaining ingredients. Cook on low for 8 hours or on high for 4 hours.

Place roast on a cutting board, let rest a few minutes, then shred using two forks. Serve as is or on buns with coleslaw.

"You cannot truly say you live well if you don't eat well."
Nigella Lawson

Potato Chip Tilapia

6 cups regular potato chips (or sour cream/onion),
finely crushed

2 T. chopped fresh dill (or 2 tsp. dried dill), divided

2 T. fresh parsley, divided

1/3 cup light mayonnaise

2 tsp. spicy brown mustard

2-3 cloves garlic, minced

4 tilapia fillets

Lemon wedges, optional

Preheat oven to 425 degrees. Coat baking sheet with cooking
spray. Combine crushed chips with one tablespoon fresh dill
or one teaspoon dried. Reserve one tablespoon parsley and
dill.

In small bowl combine mayonnaise, mustard, garlic, and
remaining dill and parsley. Place tilapia filets on baking sheet.
Spread top with mayonnaise mixture and sprinkle each with
potato chip mixture. Pat gently to adhere.

Bake 10-12 minutes or until topping is golden brown and fish
is cooked through. Serve with lemon slices if desired.

Rosemary Pork Chops

1 1/2 cups dry bread crumbs

1/2 cup All-purpose flour

1 1/2 tsp. salt

1 to 1 ½ tsp. dried rosemary

1 tsp. paprika

¼ tsp. onion powder

3 T. vegetable or canola oil

4-6 bone-in pork loin chops, half inch thick

Cooking oil for frying

In a bowl, combine the first six dry ingredients. Stir in oil until crumbly.

Rinse and drain pork chops. Place coating mix in a bowl or a re-sealable plastic bag. Place a small amount of water in a shallow bowl. Dip pork chops in water, and then in coating mix. If using a bag, place wet pork chops in the bag and shake to coat.

In a skillet, cook chops in canola oil over medium heat for 4-5 minutes per side or until juices run clear. These are amazing!

Serves: 4

Salmon Patties

2 14-oz. cans salmon

2 T. milk (may use skim milk)

3 eggs, lightly beaten

1 tsp. Worcestershire sauce

½ tsp. dry mustard

1 ½ cups saltine crackers (about 25 crackers)

1 green pepper, chopped

½ large white onion, chopped

1 T. parsley

1-2 cloves garlic

½ tsp. salt

¼ tsp pepper

2 tablespoons olive oil

Whisk the eggs, milk, Worcestershire sauce and dry mustard. Stir in the salmon, crushed crackers, green pepper, onion, and remaining ingredients. Cover and chill for 20 minutes so patties will hold together.

Shape the salmon mixture into round patties, about 4 inches in diameter and 1/2-inch thick. Cook in oil over medium heat, about five minutes per side. Flip over using a wide spatula. These are amazing! Serves: 4

Secret-Ingredient Roast

1 chuck roast (arm roast or whatever cut you have)

½ bag carrots

1 can cream of Mushroom soup

1 packet dry onion soup mix

Salt & pepper

3/4 cup of brewed coffee

Rinse off carrots and place them in the bottom of a slow cooker. Add the roast and pour one-half cup of brewed coffee straight from the coffee pot over the meat. This is the secret ingredient! Coffee helps to tenderize the roast, as well as brown it. (My former, late mother-in-law gave me this tip!) Sprinkle the roast generously with salt and pepper, spread mushroom soup on top, and add the dry onion soup. Rinse your hands and flick water drops over the dry onion soup. Otherwise, it'll come out looking like sawdust!

Cook on low for 7-8 hours or on high for 4 hours. Remove the roast and let it set ten minutes before carving. Note: It's usually so tender it falls apart! Meanwhile, remove the carrots using a slotted spoon and serve the juice as gravy over the roast and vegetables. Easy and delicious. I usually serve this with mashed potatoes or green beans. Serves: 8-10

Sesame Salmon

1-2 lb. salmon filet

2 T. soy sauce

2 T. cider vinegar

1 T. honey

1 tsp. vegetable or canola oil

1 tsp. spicy brown mustard

¼ tsp. ground ginger

2 T. sesame seeds, toasted

3 green onions, chopped

Preheat oven to 400 degrees. Combine soy sauce, vinegar, honey, oil, mustard and ginger. Pour over salmon. Refrigerate for one hour, covered. Drain and discard marinade.

Bake for 15-20 minutes or until the fish flakes easily with a fork. Sprinkle with sesame seeds and onions.

Serves: 4

Sirloin & Herb Butter

4 beef sirloin steaks, 6-8 oz. each

4 T. butter, softened

2 cloves garlic, chopped

¼ cup finely chopped chives, parsley or basil

1 T. canola or olive oil

Combine softened butter, garlic, and herbs in a small bowl. Mix well and place in the refrigerator until firm.

Cook beef in skillet with oil several minutes per side until browned. Let stand five minutes. Top with herbed butter.

Serves: 4

"The only time to eat diet food is while you're waiting for the steak to cook." Julia Child

Spinach & Ham Carbonara Pasta

8 oz. uncooked bowtie pasta

1 ½ cups regular (or skim) milk

1 envelope carbonara pasta sauce mix (or creamy pesto)

1 ½ cups cooked ham, diced

1 10 oz. package frozen spinach, thawed and drained

Cook pasta according to package directions. In a saucepan, whisk milk and pasta sauce until blended. Bring to a low boil over medium heat, stirring constantly.

Drain pasta and stir in sauce. Add ham and spinach. Stir until heated through.

Serves: 4

**"I cook with wine. Sometimes I even add it to the food."
W.C. Fields**

Taco Lasagna

1 lb. hamburger

1 pkg. taco seasoning

1 can Rotel tomatoes (mild with green chilies)

1 can tomato sauce or taco sauce

6-8 flour tortilla shells

1 pint sour cream

1 ½ cup shredded cheddar cheese, divided

1 small jar salsa

Black olives (optional)

Preheat oven to 350 degrees. Brown hamburger. Add taco seasoning, tomato sauce, and Rotel tomatoes.

Layer tortilla shells in a greased 9 inch by 13 pan, covering the bottom and up the sides. Spoon hamburger mixture on top.

Layer the sour cream, shredded cheese, and black olives. Top with 3-4 more tortillas. Spread salsa on top and remaining cheese. Bake for 15 to 20 minutes. My mom made this and it's so good!

Serves: 8-10

Tangy Pork Chops

4 to 6 pork chops

¾ cup white vinegar

½ cup ketchup

2 T. sugar (or maple syrup—may use sugar free)

2 T. Worcestershire sauce

½ tsp. hot sauce

1 clove garlic, minced

1 tsp. ground mustard

1 tsp. paprika

1 tsp. salt

¼ tsp. pepper

½ tsp. celery seed

Rinse and place pork chops in slow cooker. Combine remaining ingredients in a mixing bowl. Stir well and pour over pork chops. Cook on low six hours. Delicious and so easy! Don't worry if you're missing some ingredients. No one will notice. This recipe also works for ribs.

Serves: 4

Turkey Breast with Orange Sauce

1 2-3 lb. sliced turkey breast

1 onion, chopped

3 garlic cloves, minced

½ tsp. dried rosemary

1 tsp. parsley

½ tsp. basil

½ tsp. sage

½ tsp. thyme

½ tsp. pepper

1 tsp. salt

1 cup orange juice

Place chopped onions in slow cooker. Place sliced turkey on top of onions and pour orange juice over the top.

Combine dry seasonings in a bowl. Mix well and place herb mixture between the turkey slices. Cover and cook on low 6-7 hours. This is absolutely delicious, moist, and looks impressive, to boot! This is my new, favorite recipe. We ate it three days in a row during quarantine, oohing and ahhing the entire time.

Serves: 6

Meatless Meals

Artichoke Quiche

1 9-inch deep-dish pastry shell

2 6-oz. jars marinated artichoke hearts

1 small onion, chopped

2 cloves garlic, minced

4 eggs

¼ cup dry bread crumbs

½ tsp. salt

¼ tsp. pepper

¼ tsp. oregano

¼ tsp. Tabasco sauce

2 cups cheddar cheese

2 T. parsley

Preheat oven to 350 degrees. Bake pie shell for 7 minutes and remove from oven. Reduce temperature to 325 degrees.

Drain artichokes and reserve marinade. Sauté onion and garlic in liquid marinade for five minutes. Whisk eggs. Stir in bread crumbs, Tabasco, and seasonings. Add cheese, artichokes, onion, and garlic. Pour all into pie shell.

Bake for 40-45 minutes until a knife inserted comes out clean.

Serves: 6-8

Baked Spinach Ravioli

2 cups spaghetti sauce

1 25-oz. pkg. frozen Italian sausage ravioli or cheese ravioli

1-2 cups shredded part-skim mozzarella cheese

½-1 package frozen chopped spinach, thawed and squeezed dry

1/4 cup grated parmesan cheese

1-2 T. garlic, chopped

Preheat oven to 350 degrees. Place one cup spaghetti sauce in a greased shallow 2 quart baking dish. Top with half of the frozen ravioli and layer with mozzarella cheese, spinach, garlic, and parmesan cheese. Repeat layers.

Bake uncovered for 40-45 minutes or until heated through and cheese is melted. This dish which begins with frozen pasta will look as though you were in the kitchen all afternoon. It's so easy and delicious. Serve with garlic bread and salad.

Serves: 8

"Life is a combination of magic and pasta."
Federico Fellini

Bean and Cheese Quesadilla

2 soft tortilla shells (flour or corn)

½ can refried beans

¼ c Cheddar cheese, shredded

Salsa, guacamole, or sour cream

Lettuce (if you still have fresh produce)

Place tortilla shell in a pan on low heat. When slightly browned turn over using tongs. Spread refried beans on the shell to within half an inch of the outer edge. Add cheddar cheese and top with another tortilla shell. Heat until lightly browned and cheese is melted. Repeat for a second serving.

Slice vertically and horizontally using a pizza cutter so you have pie-shaped wedges. Top with whatever you have on hand—salsa, guacamole, sour cream, or lettuce. Simple and delicious.

Serves 1-2 (double or triple for more people)

Butternut Squash Parmesan

1 butternut squash

1 T. olive oil

2 garlic cloves

½ cup pecans, chopped

2/3 cup parmesan cheese

2-3 scallions

½ tsp. chili flakes

1 tsp. salt

Preheat oven to 350 degrees. Halve squash and scoop out seeds. Slice into cubes and place in a cooking pan.

Mix garlic and olive oil and place in a skillet. Bring to a simmer. Spoon over sliced squash.

In a small bowl, mix pecans, parmesan cheese, a dash of olive oil, chili flakes, salt, and scallions. Spread mixture on top of squash. Bake for 20 minutes.

"Your diet is a bank account. Good food choices are good investments." Bethenny Frankel

Egg and Cheese Quesadilla

2 soft tortilla shells (flour or corn)

2 eggs, scrambled

¼ c Cheddar cheese, shredded

Salsa

Scramble egg separately. I add one teaspoon of water to make them fluffier. Also, add salt and pepper to taste.

Place tortilla shell in a pan on low heat. When slightly browned turn over using tongs. Spread cooked eggs on the shell to within half an inch of the outer edge. Add cheddar cheese and top with another tortilla shell. Heat on both sides until lightly browned and cheese is melted.

Slice vertically and horizontally using a pizza cutter for pie-shaped wedges. Top with salsa and enjoy.

Serves: 1-2 (double for more people)

Garlic Spaghetti

1 package spaghetti

6 garlic cloves, minced

12 cup olive oil

½ cup fresh parsley, minced (dried parsley will work)

2 T. pine nuts

½ tsp. salt

¼ tsp. pepper

Cook spaghetti according to package directions. In a large skillet, brown garlic and pine nuts in oil over medium heat, 1-2 minutes. Remove from heat.

Drain spaghetti and add to the skillet. Add parsley, salt, and pepper. Toss to coat and keep warm until serving.

Serves: 4-6

"Everything you see I owe to spaghetti." Sophia Loren

Manicotti

12 large manicotti shells

4 cups shredded mozzarella cheese, divided

2 cups ricotta cheese (cottage cheese will work)

6 T. fresh basil, chopped (or 2 tablespoons dried basil)

1 26-oz. jar spaghetti sauce, divided

½ cup grated parmesan or Romano cheese

Preheat oven to 350 degrees. Grease 9 by 13 casserole dish. Cook pasta according to package directions. Drain and rinse with cool water. Dry on paper towels.

Prepare filling. Stir together 3 cups of mozzarella with the ricotta and basil. Using a teaspoon, carefully stuff pasta shells with cheese mixture.

Add 2 cups spaghetti into bottom of baking dish. Arrange stuffed pasta on top. Pour remaining spaghetti sauce over top. Sprinkle with 1 cup mozzarella. Bake for 15 minutes. Sprinkle with parmesan or Romano cheese.

Serves: 6

Pasta & Peas

½-1 package bowtie or rotini pasta

1 jar of your favorite red or white pasta sauce

¼ - ½ pkg. frozen peas or broccoli, thawed

¼ cup parmesan cheese

Add water to a large pot. Sprinkle with several shakes of salt. Bring to a boil. Add the pasta and cook 9-12 minutes, depending on how firm you prefer your pasta.

In a smaller pot, heat your favorite red or white sauce. These are great pantry items to stock up on. If you're using peas or broccoli, add them to the sauce and heat through.

Drain spaghetti in a colander, add pasta sauce, and enjoy with toasted garlic bread. Easy peasy.

Serves: 2-4

"Vegetables are a must on a diet. I suggest carrot cake, zucchini bread and pumpkin pie." Jim Davis

Pasta Con Broccoli

1 cup butter

¾ cup parmesan cheese (grated or shredded)

1 T. milk

1 pint heavy whipping cream

3/4 to 1 package shell pasta

¼ tsp. crushed red pepper

3-4 cloves garlic, diced

2 cups broccoli

Parmesan cheese (to garnish)

Parsley (to garnish)

Prepare pasta according to package directions. Meanwhile melt butter in a large pot. Reduce heat and add milk, cream, garlic, broccoli, and seasonings. Stir well.

After draining pasta, add to pot with broccoli and seasonings. Coat and serve while hot. (If you don't have all of these ingredients, just use what you have. You may also substitute peas or mushrooms for the broccoli.)

Serves: 4

Sage Ravioli

One package cheese ravioli, fresh or frozen

¼ cup fresh sage leaves (or 1 ½ teaspoons dried sage)

4 T. butter

¼ cup bread crumbs

Cook ravioli according to package directions. Choose the shortest cooking time for al dente pasta. Drain and set aside.

Add butter in a large skillet until melted. Add ravioli, bread crumbs, and sage until toasted.

Serves: 2

"After a good dinner one can forgive anybody, even one's own relations." Oscar Wilde

Spinach Lasagna

1 16-oz. carton cottage cheese

1 pkg. frozen chopped spinach, thawed and drained

3 cups shredded mozzarella cheese, divided

2 eggs, whisked

1 26-oz. jar spaghetti sauce, divided

9 lasagna noodles, cooked and drained

Preheat oven to 350 degrees. Prepare lasagna according to package directions, drain, and cool.

Mix cottage cheese, spinach, 2 cups of the mozzarella cheese, one fourth cup of the parmesan cheese, and eggs.

Using a 9 x 13 baking dish, layer one cup of the spaghetti sauce, three cooked lasagna noodles, and half of the cottage cheese mixture. Repeat layers finishing with the two cheeses.

Bake for 45 minutes.

Serves: 8-10

Stir Fry with Cashews

1 head broccoli

1 head cauliflower

1/3 bag carrots

1 medium onion (white or yellow)

1 red pepper

½ - 1 cup cashews

Soy Sauce

Stir Fry Sauce

Rice, cooked separately

Chop broccoli and cauliflower in one-inch pieces. Slice carrots into half unless they're small. Chop onion and red pepper into one-inch pieces.

Place the broccoli, cauliflower, and carrots in a pre-heated pan with vegetable, olive, or canola oil. Cook for 5 minutes on medium high heat, stirring and flipping over with a spatula to cook evenly. Add onion and red pepper. Sauté another 15 minutes while continuing to stir. Add cashews for protein. Top with your favorite stir fry sauce for another minute or two.

Serve over hot, cooked rice. Egg rolls make an excellent side dish. Serves: 2-4

Stuffed Jumbo Pasta Shells

1 12-oz. package jumbo pasta shells, cooked

2 to 3 cups shredded mozzarella cheese

1 15-oz. carton ricotta cheese

1 10-oz. pkg. frozen chopped spinach, thawed and cooked

3 garlic cloves, minced

½ tsp. basil

½ tsp. oregano

¼ tsp. red pepper flakes (optional)

1 large jar spaghetti sauce

Preheat oven to 350 degrees. Combine cheeses, spices, and cooked spinach. Arrange cooked pasta shells in a greased 9 by 13 baking dish. Stuff shells with cheese mixture. May have extra. Use a smaller pan for leftovers or freeze at this point.

Pour spaghetti sauce over the shells and bake for 30 minutes. Check at the halfway mark and cover with foil if getting too brown. This makes a beautiful presentation!

Serves: 10 to 12

Vegetable Primavera

½ bag rotini (corkscrew pasta)

½ head broccoli

½ head cauliflower

1 onion

1 bell pepper

1 yellow squash or zucchini

1 tsp. basil

1 tsp. oregano

24 oz. jar red spaghetti sauce (use your favorite brand)

¼ cup parmesan cheese

Cook pasta according to package directions. Sauté the vegetables in a frying pan using vegetable or canola oil for ten minutes. Season with spices and leave crispy.

Heat the sauce separately on medium heat.

Place pasta in an ungreased 9" x 13" casserole dish. Top with sauce, then add vegetables. Sprinkle with grated Parmesan cheese to taste. May heat in the microwave before serving.

Serves: 8-10

Candy, Cookies & Bars

Banana Raisin Cookies

3 ripe bananas, mashed

1/3 cup applesauce

2 cups oats

1/4 cup almond or coconut milk

1/2 cup raisins

1 tsp. vanilla

1 tsp. cinnamon

1/4 cup pecans, chopped

Preheat oven to 350 degrees. Peel and mash bananas using a fork. Mix all ingredients in a mixing bowl. Fold in bananas.

Form into 2-inch balls and place on greased cookie sheet. Bake 15-20 minutes.

Chocolate Peanut Butter Balls

1 ¼ cups graham cracker crumbs

1 ½ cups peanut butter (may use cashew or almond butter)

1 lb. powdered sugar

2 sticks butter, melted

½ stick paraffin

Using a large bowl, pour melted butter over first 3 ingredients. Form walnut-sized mounds and place balls onto waxed paper. Let set.

In a double boiler, melt the chocolate chips and half a stick of paraffin until smooth. Drop peanut butter balls in the chocolate mixture and remove using a spoon. Place onto wax paper and let set. These are delicious. Store in airtight containers or holiday tins.

Yield: 50

"One cannot think well, love well, sleep well, if one has not dined well." Virginia Woolf

Chocolate-Covered Cashew Clusters

1/2 package chocolate almond bark

12 oz. chocolate chips

10-12 oz. cashews (or peanuts)

Melt almond bark in microwave 1-2 minutes. Add chocolate chips and melt another minute. Remove from microwave and stir in peanuts or cashews. Drop 2" mounds onto waxed paper and let set.

These three ingredients pack a punch. They're my dad's favorite candy (mine too!) Store in airtight containers for up to a week.

Yield: 40 clusters

Coconut Fruit Balls

1 cup coconut

½ - 1 cup pecans

1 cup dried cranberries (or dried apricots)

1 cup Eagle Brand milk (fat free is fine)

1 cup oats

1 cup raisins

Splash orange juice

½ cup chocolate chips, optional

Mix first 6 ingredients in a bowl. Use whatever ingredients you have on hand. Add chocolate chips if you prefer sweeter candy. Add a tablespoon of orange juice, if desired. I like the chocolate and orange combination.

Mixture will be sticky. If it's too wet, simply add more oats and/or coconut. Roll into 1" or 2" balls and bake at 325 degrees for 13 minutes. These are akin to round granola bars and make a healthy snack. Get the kids or grandkids involved!

Yield: 30-35 balls

Haystacks

2 cups peanuts (or cashews)

2 cups chow mein noodles

12 oz. pkg butterscotch morsels

Using a microwave-safe dish, melt morsels in microwave for 1-2 minutes, until melted. Stir in peanuts or cashews and chow mein noodles. Drop onto waxed paper until set.

Yield: 30

"My doctor told me I had to stop throwing intimate dinners for four unless there are three other people."
Orson Welles

Lemon Cookies

1 box lemon cake mix

4 oz. Cool Whip

1 egg

½ cup powdered sugar

Preheat oven to 325 degrees. Mix first three ingredients together (will be thick.) Form walnut-size balls and roll in powdered sugar.

Bake for 10 minutes or until top cracks.

Optional: May use a chocolate cake mix if you're, gasp, not a lemon fan.

"Home is the place where, when you have to go there, they have to take you in." Robert Frost

No-Bake Cookies

2 cups white sugar

4 tsp. cocoa

3 ½ cups quick oats

½ cup milk

1 stick butter

½ cup peanut butter (or cashew butter)

Boil sugar, cocoa, and butter for 1 ½ minutes. Stir in milk. Remove from heat and add peanut butter and oats. Stir quickly as these tend to set up fast. Drop onto waxed paper and let cool.

Potato Chip Cookies

2 sticks butter, softened

2/3 cup sugar (or Splenda)

1 tsp. vanilla

1 ½ cups all-purpose flour

½ cup regular potato chips, crushed

Preheat oven to 350 degrees. Cream butter, sugar, and vanilla. Stir in flour. Carefully fold in crushed potato chips.

Drop by spoonful onto an ungreased baking sheet. Bake for 10-12 minutes or until lightly browned.

"A balanced diet is a cookie in each hand." Barbara Johnson

Spice Cake Oatmeal Cookies

1 package spice cake mix

4 egg whites

1 cup quick cooking oats, uncooked

½ cup canola or vegetable oil

½ cup raisins

½ cup pecans (optional)

Preheat oven to 350 degrees. Combine cake mix, egg whites, oats, and oil. Beat on low speed until blended. Stir in raisins and nuts. Drop by rounded teaspoons onto greased baking sheet.

Bake 7-9 minutes or until lightly browned. Cool five minutes and remove to platter or cooling racks.

Yield: 48 cookies

Strawberry Cream Cheese Bars

1 strawberry cake mix

1 stick butter

3 eggs, divided

1 8-oz. package cream cheese, softened

2 cups powdered sugar

Preheat oven to 325 degrees. In large mixing bowl, combine cake mix, butter, and one egg. Blend well. Press mixture into bottom of greased 9 x 13 baking dish.

In smaller bowl, mix cream cheese, 2 eggs, and powdered sugar. Blend 1-2 minutes until smooth. Pour mixture over cake batter. Bake 30-35 minutes or until lightly browned. Cool and cut into squares.

Serves: 12

Texas Gold Bars

Crust:

    1 box yellow cake mix

    1 egg

    1 stick butter, melted

Topping:

    1 8 o. pkg. cream cheese

    2 eggs

    1 lb. powdered sugar

Preheat oven to 375 degrees. Mix cake mix, one egg, and butter together. Beat until smooth. Pat dough into a 9 x 13 cake pan.

Combine cream cheese, two eggs, and powdered sugar. Mix well and pour over crust.

Bake 35 minutes. Let cool for two hours and cut into bars.

Quarantine Balls

(a/k/a Peanut Butter Balls)

½ cup peanut butter (low-fat is fine)

2 ripe bananas, smashed

2 cups oats

Combine peanut butter and oats. Add bananas until moistened. Roll into balls. Bake at 350 degrees on ungreased cookie sheet for 15 minutes.

NOTE: May substitute almond butter or cashew butter for the peanut butter.

Yield: 24 balls

"The way I see it, if you want the rainbow, you gotta put up with the rain." Dolly Parton

Desserts

Banana Fudge Layer Cake

1 package yellow cake mix

3 eggs

1 1/3 cups water

1/3 cup vegetable or canola oil

3 ripe bananas, mashed

1 container chocolate frosting

Preheat oven to 350 degrees. Grease and flour two round cake pans. Combine cake mix, eggs, water, and oil. Beat on low speed until moistened. Beat on medium speed for two more minutes. Add mashed bananas and stir well.

Pour into pans. Bake for 27-30 minutes or until a toothpick inserted comes out clean. Cool fifteen minutes before removing from pans. After cakes are cool, frost with chocolate frosting.

Serves: 12

Banana Rum Cake

1 box yellow cake mix

1/8 tsp. baking soda

2 eggs

1/3 cup chopped pecans

2/3 cup light rum

2/3 cup water

1 ripe banana, mashed

Preheat oven to 350 degrees. Grease and flour 2 nine-inch cake pans or one 9 x 13 cake pan. Combine all ingredients in a large bowl. Blend well.

Pour into pans and bake 25-30 minutes. When cool, dust with powdered sugar.

Serves: 12

Banana Split Cake

5 bananas

2 sticks butter, divided

3 cups crushed graham crackers

2 eggs

2 cups powdered sugar

8 oz. cream cheese

1 T. vanilla

1 16 oz. can crushed pineapple, drained

1 large container Cool Whip

1 small jar maraschino cherries

1 small package chopped pecans or walnuts

Melt one stick butter and mix with graham cracker crumbs. Press into 13 by 9 by 2 1/2 inch pan.

Beat one stick butter, 2 eggs, cream cheese, two cups powdered sugar, and vanilla until fluffy. Spread over cracker crust.

Cover with bananas, sliced lengthwise, then cover with drained pineapple. Top with Cool Whip and sprinkle with chopped nuts and cherries.

Refrigerate several hours or overnight. This is great in the summer.

Serves: 12

Better-Than-Almost-Anything Cake

1 box German chocolate cake mix

(Add water, oil and eggs as directed on cake mix package)

1 14-oz. can sweetened condensed milk

1 17-oz. jar caramel or fudge topping (may use less fat)

8 oz. Cool Whip, thawed

1 8 oz. bag toffee bits

1 small jar Maraschino Cherries

Preheat oven to 350 degrees. Bake cake as directed on package and spread in a 9 x 13 pan. Cool 15 minutes.

Using the handle of a wooden spoon, poke top of warm cake every 1/2 inch. Drizzle sweetened condensed milk evenly over top of cake. Wait until milk has been absorbed. Drizzle with caramel topping.

Cover and refrigerate two hours or until chilled. Spread Cool Whip over cake. Top with maraschino cherries and nuts.

Serves: 12

"Seize the moment. Remember all those women on the 'Titanic' who waved off the dessert cart." Erma Bombeck

Black Forest Cherry Dump Cake

1 can cherry pie filling

1 can pitted dark cherries, drained

1 German chocolate cake mix

1 regular (or diet) cherry Cola

Preheat oven to 350 degrees. Grease a 9 by 13 pan. Spread cherry pie filling over the bottom. Sprinkle with pitted cherries. Add cake mix and use a fork or spoon to spread evenly. Pour soda over the cake mix.

Bake 40 to 45 minutes. This looks like fancy brownies and doesn't use eggs nor oil! Amazing.

Serves: 12

Blueberry Angel Food Trifle

1 prepared Angel food cake, cubed

1 can blueberry pie filling

1 pkg. lemon pudding (may usc sugar free)

1 8 oz. tub Cool Whip

Cube angel food cake into two-inch pieces. Prepare lemon pudding according to package directions.

Using a large, glass bowl (to show the layers!) place cake on the bottom, followed by half a can of pie filling, half the pudding, and half the Cool Whip. Repeat layers.

Refrigerate a few hours or overnight.

NOTE: This is also pretty in parfait glasses and is a simple dessert.

Serves: 10-12

Brownie Pie

1 package brownie mix

2 eggs

½ cup vegetable or canola oil

¼ cup water

½ cup semi-sweet chocolate chips

1 deep-dish pastry shell

Preheat oven to 350 degrees. Combine brownie mix, eggs, oil, add water in a large bowl until blended. Stir in chocolate chips. Spoon mixture into pie crust.

Bake 40-45 minutes or until set. Check pie after 30 minutes. You may need to put foil around the edges to prevent too much browning.

Cool and serve with vanilla ice cream or strawberries. There's something about this pretty pie that tastes so much better than a pan of brownies (if that's possible!)

Serves: 4-6

Carrot Pineapple Cake

1 carrot cake mix

½ cup water

½ cup canola oil

4 eggs, whisked

1 8-oz. can crushed pineapple, undrained

½ cup pecans, chopped

½ cup coconut

½ cup raisins (2 small boxes)

Preheat oven to 350 degrees. Grease 9 by 13 cake pan. Beat cake mix, water, oil, eggs, and pineapple in a large bowl on low speed for 30 seconds. Beat on medium for 2 minutes.

Bake for 37-42 minutes. Allow to cool completely before frosting.

Cream Cheese Frosting

1 8 oz. package cream cheese (may use fat-free)

¼ cup butter, softened

2-3 tsp. milk

1 tsp. vanilla

3 cups powdered sugar

Beat cream cheese, butter, milk, and vanilla on low until smooth. Gradually add powdered sugar until spreadable. Spread on cake and store in the refrigerator. Serves: 12

Cherry Dump Cake

1 20-oz. can crushed pineapple with juice

1 can cherry pie filling (or blueberry)

1 yellow cake mix

½ - 1 cup pecans, chopped

½ cup butter, melted

Preheat oven to 350 degrees. Grease a 9 by 13-inch cake pan. Dump pineapple with juice into pan and spread evenly. Spread cherry pie filling on top. Add cake mix evenly over the top and sprinkle with chopped pecans.

Melt butter for 30-40 seconds in the microwave. Spread over the cake to moisten. Bake 45-40 minutes. This recipe doesn't have a pretty name, but it's easy and delicious. Serve warm or at room temperature by itself or with vanilla ice cream.

Serves: 12

"Just try to be angry with someone who fed you something delicious." Carmen Cook

Chocolate Chip Pie

2 eggs, whisked

½ cup flour

1 cup sugar

1 stick butter, melted

1 tsp. vanilla

½ cup semi-sweet chocolate chips

½ cup pecans

Frozen pie shell, thawed

Preheat oven to 350 degrees. Mix all ingredients and pour into pie shell. Bake for 30 to 40 minutes. This is so good!

Serves: 8

Chocolate Ice Cream Pie

2 quarts vanilla ice cream, melted

1 5.9 oz. instant chocolate pudding mix

2 graham cracker crusts

Cool Whip, optional

In a bowl, whisk melted ice cream and pudding mix for two minutes. Pour into graham cracker crusts. Freeze until firm.

Before serving, remove from freezer for 5-10 minutes to soften. Garnish with whipped topping if desired.

Yield: 2 pies

"All you need is love. But a little chocolate now and then doesn't hurt." Charles M. Schulz

Chocolate Rum Pecan Pie

3 eggs

1/4 cup, plus 2 T. butter, melted

3/4 cup light corn syrup

1/2 cup sugar (Splenda is fine)

1/4 cup firmly packed brown sugar (Splenda works)

2 T. Rum

1 T. all-purpose flour

1 tsp. vanilla extract

1 cup chopped pecans

1 cup semi-sweet chocolate chips

1 9-inch deep dish pie shell (unbaked)

Preheat oven to 350 degrees. Beat the eggs until frothy in a large mixing bowl. Add butter, beating well. Combine syrup, sugar, brown sugar, rum, flour, and vanilla. Beat well for 1-2 minutes. Stir in chopped pecans.

Sprinkle the chocolate chips in unbaked pie shell. Pour pecan mixture over chocolate morsels. Bake for 45 to 50 minutes or until set. (If pie browns too quickly cover with foil last ten minutes.) This is downright sinful! Serves: 8

Classic Pecan Pie

3 eggs, slightly beaten

1 cup Karo light corn syrup

1 cup sugar (or 1/2 cup Splenda blend)

2 T. butter, melted

1 tsp. vanilla

1 ½ cups pecans

1 deep dish pie crust

Preheat oven to 350 degrees. In a large bowl, mix eggs, corn syrup, butter, sugar, and vanilla until well blended. Stir in pecans. Pour into pie crust. Bake 45 to 50 minutes, or until knife inserted halfway between center and edge comes out clean. Cool on wire rack.

Serves: 8

Fluffy Pineapple Pie

8-10 oz. crushed pineapple in its own juice, drained

1 small pkg. lemon Jello (sugar free is fine)

12 oz. Cool Whip

Graham cracker or shortbread pie crust

Stir the drained pineapple and Jello together. Fold in the Cool Whip. Spoon into store-bought crust and refrigerate for a few hours.

This is a simple and refreshing pie.

Serves: 8

"Life is uncertain. Eat dessert first." Ernestine Ulmer

Fourth of July Dessert

1 frozen pound cake, thawed

½ can blueberry pie filling

½ can strawberry pie filling

1 8 oz. carton whipped topping, thawed

Slice cake horizontally into three layers. Place bottom layer on a serving plate. Spread with the blueberry filling. Add second layer of cake and spread with strawberry pie filling. Top with third layer of cake.

Frost top and sides with whipped topping. Chill several hours or overnight. This is simple and looks festive!

Serves: 8

Ice Cream Sandwich Cake

21 mini ice cream sandwiches (or 19 full size sandwiches) – sugar-free works too!

1 12-oz. carton Cool Whip, thawed

1 jar hot fudge ice cream topping

1 cup cashews (or peanuts)

Place ice cream sandwiches in an ungreased 9 x 13 cake pan. Arrange along the sides, top, and place side by side, until there is no space in between. Note: You may need to cut some in half to make them fit.

Spread ice cream sandwiches with half of the whipped topping. Top with fudge topping and sprinkle ½ cup of the nuts. Repeat layers.

Cover and freeze overnight. Remove from the freezer ten minutes before serving. This is such a fun, unique summer dessert! Kids and grands will especially love it, but so do adults.

Serves: 12

Key Lime Pie

1 graham cracker pie crust

1 4-oz. sugar free (or regular) lime-flavored gelatin

¼ cup boiling water

2 6-oz. containers Key Lime pie-flavored yogurt

1 8-oz. tub Cool Whip, thawed

Boil water in small saucepan. In a large heat-resistant bowl, add gelatin and boiling water. Stir well. Add yogurt and whisk until smooth. Fold in whipped topping and spread in pie crust. Refrigerate overnight or for three hours.

Serves: 6-8

"I don't share blame. I don't share credit. And I don't share desserts." Beverly Sills

Mint Chocolate Ice Cream Pie

1/2 gallon mint chocolate chip ice cream

1 store-bought chocolate pie crust

Soften ice cream for 20 minutes. Spoon into pie crust and smooth the top. Cover with plastic wrap and freeze overnight. This simple recipe has gotten so many rave reviews! Mix and match using different ice cream and crusts.

Other ice cream pie options:

Cherry chip ice cream

Shortbread or chocolate pie crust

Butter pecan ice cream

Shortbread or graham cracker pie crust

Use your imagination. The possibilities are endless. You will love this easy dessert.

Minty Brownies

1 brownie mix

½ bag of mint patties

Prepare your favorite brownie mix according to package directions. Pour half the batter into a greased 9 x 11 pan. Top with mints. Add remaining batter and bake as directed on package.

Serves: 10-12

"With the new day, comes new strength and new thoughts." Eleanor Roosevelt

Mississippi Mud Cake

2 sticks butter, melted

1/3 cup cocoa

1 cup coconut

1 ½ cups pecans

4 eggs, whisked

2 cups sugar

1 ½ cups flour

1 jar marshmallow cream

Preheat oven to 325 degrees. Mix butter, sugar, eggs, flour, and cocoa. Beat well for two minutes. Stir in nuts and coconut. Mix well and spread into a greased 9 x 13 pan. Bake 35-40 minutes. Remove from the oven and spread a jar of marshmallow cream on top. Then, add icing:

1 box powdered sugar

1/3 cup cocoa

½ cup butter, melted

1 tsp. vanilla

1-2 tsp. milk, as needed if too thick

Mix icing ingredients and beat until smooth. Spoon dollops on top of cake while cake is hot. The icing and marshmallow cream will run together and make swirls. Serves: 12

Oatmeal Cake

1 1/4 cups boiling water

1 cup oats, uncooked

1/2 cup butter

1 cup sugar

1 cup brown sugar

1 tsp. vanilla

2 eggs

1 1/3 cups flour

1 tsp. soda

1/2 tsp. salt

1 tsp. cinnamon

1/4 tsp. nutmeg

Preheat oven to 350 degrees. Add oats to boiling water (let oats stand in water for 20 minutes.) Cream butter, sugar, vanilla, and eggs. Sift flour, soda and salt. Add to butter mixture. Mix well and add to oatmeal, adding cinnamon and nutmeg. Stir well. Bake in a greased 9 x 13 cake pan for 30 minutes. Meanwhile, make frosting:

1/4 cup butter, melted

1 egg

1 cup brown sugar

(continued)

1 cup coconut

3 T. canned, evaporated milk

½ - 1 cup pecans

1/2 tsp. vanilla

Whisk butter and eggs. Stir in remaining ingredients, adding nuts and coconuts last. Mix well. Spread on hot cake. Return to oven and broil 2 to 2 1/2 minutes until coconut is toasted. Serves: 12

Peach Crumble

1 can peach pie filling (or use cherry!)

½ cup quick cooking oats

½ cup flour

½ cup brown sugar, firmly packed

1 stick butter, melted

¼ tsp. cinnamon

Preheat oven to 350 degrees. Pour pie filling into a greased 8 x 8 baking dish. In a mixing bowl, combine oats, flour, brown sugar, and cinnamon. Add butter until mixture is coarse and thoroughly blended. Sprinkle dry mixture over pie filling.

Bake 40 to 45 minutes.

Serves: 6

"I'm not gaining weight. I'm retaining food." Author Unknown

Peanut Butter Pie

3 oz. cream cheese, softened (I use fat-free)

½ cup crunchy peanut butter

1 cup powdered sugar, sifted (or not!)

1 tub of Cool Whip

1 graham cracker crust

Mix first three ingredients in a large bowl until blended. Add Cool Whip and pour into a graham cracker crust. Freeze. Before serving, let set a few minutes to soften.

You will not believe how delicious this is! If you have peanut allergies in your family, try using almond or cashew butter in place of the peanut butter.

Serves: 8

"Stress cannot exist in the presence of a pie." David Mamet

Pecan Pie Cake

1 yellow cake mix

4 eggs, divided

1/2 cup butter, melted

1 1/2 cups white Karo corn syrup

1/2 cup dark brown sugar, packed (may substitute Splenda)

1 tsp. vanilla extract

1-2 cups pecans, chopped

Preheat oven to 325 degrees. Mix cake mix, 1 egg, and melted butter. Reserve 2/3 cup of batter. Spread the remaining batter into a greased and floured 9 x 13 inch pan.

Bake for 15 minutes or until lightly browned. Then:

Mix reserved 2/3 cup batter with corn syrup, 3 eggs, brown sugar, vanilla, and pecans. Pour filling on top of crust and cook another 50-60 minutes.

Serves: 12

"Wringing your hands only stops you from rolling up your sleeves." James Rollins

Pina' Colada Cake

1 box yellow cake mix with pudding

½ can Eagle Brand milk

¾ can Lopez Cream of Coconut

¾ cup coconut

1 8 oz. tub Cool Whip

½ cup pecans (if desired)

Bake cake in an oblong baking dish according to package directions. When slightly cool, punch holes in the cake at 1" intervals using the handle of a wooden spoon.

Pour half a can of Eagle Brand milk on top of cake. Let stand 10 minutes. Pour ¾ can Lopez cream of coconut on cake. Sprinkle with fresh coconut and top with cool whip. This is fantastic and so easy!

Serves: 12

"Good Food is Good Mood." Anonymous

Pistachio Cake

1 box white cake mix

1 3.4 oz. pkg. instant pistachio pudding mix

3 eggs

1 cup canola oil

1 12 oz. can lemon lime soda

Frosting:

1 3.4 oz. pkg. instant pistachio pudding mix

1 1/2 cups milk

1 8 oz. container frozen whipped topping, thawed

1/4 cup chopped pistachio nuts (for garnish)

Preheat oven to 350 degrees. Grease two 9-inch round cake pans. In a large bowl, beat cake mix, pudding mix, eggs, oil, and soda on low for 1 minute and medium for 2-3 minutes. Equally divide batter between prepared cake pans. Bake for 35 minutes or until a toothpick comes out clean. Cool cake layers for 20 minutes. Turn directly onto racks and cool completely.

To prepare frosting, beat pudding mix and milk for two minutes on medium speed in a large bowl. Fold in whipped topping. Place one cake layer on a serving plate and frost top. Repeat with remaining layer. Then, frost sides and garnish with nuts, if desired. Store in refrigerator. Serves: 12

Poppy Seed Cake

1 package yellow or lemon cake mix

1 package lemon or coconut cream pudding mix

½ cup vegetable oil

3 eggs, whisked

1 ½ T. poppy seeds

1 cup water

Preheat oven to 350 degrees. In a mixing bowl, combine cake mix, water, oil, and eggs. Beat on low speed until moistened, then on medium speed for 2 minutes. Stir in poppy seeds.

Pour batter into a greased Bundt pan. Bake for 35-40 minutes. Remove from pan when cool. Dust with powdered sugar or use glaze below.

Serves: 12

Glaze:

¾ cup powdered sugar

3-4 tsp. lemon juice

2 drops yellow food coloring, optional

½ tsp. vanilla

Mix and heat in microwave 15-20 seconds. Stir and drop by spoonfuls on top of cake.

Pumpkin Rum Cake

One white (or yellow) cake mix

1 15-oz. can of pumpkin

3 eggs, whisked

½ cup rum (or coconut rum)

½ cup pecans, chopped

Preheat oven to 325 degrees. In a large mixing bowl, combine the cake mix, pumpkins, eggs, and rum. Beat on low speed for 30 seconds, then on medium for two minutes. Fold in pecans.

Bake for 45 minutes until toothpick comes out clean. Let cool before placing on a cake plate. Dust with powdered sugar or use glaze below.

Orange Glaze:

¾-1 cup powdered sugar

2 T. orange juice

1 T. orange zest

Combine powdered sugar and orange juice. Using a grater, add zest from the orange. Stir until blended and spoon over cake.

"A party without cake is just a meeting." Julia Child

Snow Ice Cream

8 cups of clean snow (or shaved ice)

1 14-oz. can sweetened condensed milk

1 tsp. vanilla

Chocolate sprinkles (optional)

Chocolate or caramel syrup (optional)

Place snow or shaved ice in a large bowl. Add condensed milk and vanilla. Mix until combined. Serve immediately. Add chocolate chips or syrup if desired. This is a fun activity if you live in a northern state or country. The kids will love it.

Serves: 8

"It's okay to play with your food." Emeril Lagasse

Sock-It-To-Me-Cake

1 box Duncan Hines butter cake mix

1/3 cup sugar (or one T. Splenda)

3/4 cup oil

8 oz. carton sour cream

4 eggs

1 tsp. vanilla

Filling:

1 1/2 tsp. cinnamon

3 T. brown sugar (Splenda works)

3 T. pecans

Preheat oven to 325 degrees. Mix cake ingredients thoroughly and pour half of batter into well-greased Bundt pan.

Combine filling ingredients until well blended. Sprinkle filling on top of cake. Add other half of cake batter. Bake 45-50 minutes and let cool before adding glaze.

Glaze:

    1/2 cup powdered sugar

    ½ T. butter, melted

    1/2 tsp. vanilla

    2/3 T. milk

Mix powdered sugar and milk first, then add other ingredients.

Strawberries & Cream Freezer Sandwiches

12-16 graham crackers

1 8-oz. tub Cool Whip

1 pint strawberries, sliced

Thaw whipped topping. In a bowl, combine strawberries and Cool Whip. Press onto one graham cracker and top with another graham cracker. Repeat.

Wrap strawberry sandwiches in plastic wrap and freeze for three hours or overnight.

Serves: 6-8

"There is no love sincerer than the love of food." George Bernard Shaw

Strawberry Pie

1 cup sugar (may use Splenda)

1 cup water

½ package wild strawberry Jell-O

1 heaping T. cornstarch

1 quart fresh sliced strawberries

1 9-inch pie shell, baked

Bake pie shell according to package directions. Allow to cool.

Combine sugar, cornstarch, and water in a small saucepan. Cook over low heat until thickened and beginning to clear. Remove from heat and add Jell-O. Stir and set aside until completely cool.

Combine liquid with strawberries and pour into baked pie shell. Refrigerate several hours or overnight until set. This is pretty and delicious! I always double the recipe for family gatherings. Optional: Top slices with Cool Whip.

Serves: 8

Strawberry Yogurt Cake

1 package white cake mix

1/3 cup canola oil

1 cup water

3 eggs

1 6-oz. container strawberry or strawberry banana yogurt

1 quart strawberries, sliced in half

Heat oven to 350 degrees. Grease 9 by 13 pan. Beat cake mix, oil, water, eggs, and yogurt in a large mixing bowl. Beat on low speed for 30 seconds and medium for 2 minutes. Pour into prepared pan.

Bake for 35 minutes. Cool completely before preparing frosting:

2-2 ½ cups powdered sugar

1/3 cup butter, softened

1 ½ tsp. vanilla

1-2 T. milk

Mix powdered sugar and butter in medium bowl on low speed. Stir in vanilla and milk. Beat until smooth. Spread on cake and top with fresh strawberries. This is my favorite cake!

Serves: 12

Two-Ingredient Pineapple Cake

One Angel food cake mix

20 oz. crushed pineapple (including the juice)

Cool Whip or vanilla ice cream

Preheat oven to 350 degrees. Mix cake mix and pineapple (including the juice) in a mixing bowl until fluffy and airy. Pour into greased cake pan.

Bake for 30 minutes. When cool, serve with Cool Whip or ice cream. NOTE: I saw this recipe on Facebook last year. It's simple and delicious.

Serves: 12

OPTIONAL: When cool, cut the cake into 2-inch cubes. Place in a glass bowl and layer with blueberry or cherry pie filling and Cool Whip for an easy, delicious trifle.

Two-Ingredient Pumpkin Muffins

1 yellow or spice cake mix

1 can of pumpkin

Optional: raisins or pecans (1/3 to 1/2 cup each)

Preheat oven to 350 degrees. Blend cake mix and pumpkin together for 2 minutes. If using raisins or pecans, stir them into the batter. Note: No eggs are needed!

Drop by heaping tablespoons into greased muffin tins. Bake for 18-22 minutes.

This is another Facebook recipe and is surprisingly tasty. I baked mine in leaf-shaped muffin tins last fall. The muffins were adorable and delicious.

Yield: 25 to 30 muffins

"Happiness is the best facelift." Diana Krall

Vanilla Cherry Trifle

One white cake mix (or yellow or Angel food)

1 can of cherry pie filling (or blueberry)

Vanilla pudding (or lemon or cheesecakc)

Cool Whip

Fresh mint for garnish (optional)

You can mix and match these ingredients to suit your needs and use whatever is in your pantry. Bake the cake according to package instructions. Let cool and cut into 1-2" chunks.

Place cake pieces in a large glass dish (or use 4-6 parfait glasses). Spread cherry pie filling over cake, top with pudding, then add Cool Whip. Repeat layers.

Serves: 4-6

NOTE: Use fresh fruit if you have it. I've even made this with sliced fresh strawberries, chocolate chips, and a drizzle of chocolate syrup. Nuts or coconut would also be good. Use your imagination and involve the kids while constructing the parfaits!

Vanilla Pineapple Cake

1 pkg. vanilla Jell-O instant pudding and pie filling

1 20-oz. can crushed pineapple, undrained

8-oz. tub whipped topping, thawed

1 10 oz. prepared angel food cake

1 cup fresh seasonal berries (strawberries, blueberries, kiwi—whatever you have!)

Mix dry pudding mix and pineapple (with juice) in medium bowl. Gently add whipped topping. Cut cake horizontally into three layers. Place bottom cake layer on a serving plate.

Top bottom layer with one third of the pudding mixture. Repeat layers twice. Refrigerate several hours.

Before serving, top with fresh berries. Store in refrigerator.

Vanilla Pineapple Mousse

Using the vanilla pudding, pineapple, and whipped topping mentioned above, mix the three together until blended. Serve in fancy glasses for an easy mousse. This works when you're in a time crunch or don't have cake or fresh fruit.

Give Yourself a Break

Let's face it, no one wants to cook every day. We're exhausted, anxious, and some are overwhelmed by homeschooling or worried about paying the bills. I say give yourself a break. Here are simple foods to eat during trying times:

- Frozen pizza

- Peanut Butter & Jelly Sandwich

- Toast with peanut butter, almond butter or cashew butter. Even better, be like Elvis and add sliced bananas on top if you still have fresh fruit.

- A bowl of cereal for those days (you know what I mean!)

- A can of soup

- Scrambled eggs

- Tuna sandwich with bread or crackers (whichever you have the most of)

- A banana, apple, orange, strawberries, or whatever you have in your fridge

- A can of fruit. My favorite is cherries.

- A handful of cashews, peanuts, almonds, or pecans

- A granola or protein bar

- Drink orange juice to get some vitamin C

- Microwave popcorn always hits the spot. Try using different seasonings to jazz it up. A unique seasoning I really enjoy is steak seasoning, which sounds weird but is tasty. Other toppings could be parmesan cheese, basil, or even cinnamon.

- I'm sure you can search your pantry or freezer and come up with quick, easy snacks or meals when you don't feel like cooking. Trust me, we all have days like that.

Non-Stir Crazy Activities

I'm reading heartbreaking reports and social media posts about people who are becoming depressed from the isolation and lack of routine. I get this. Most of us are social creatures, have jobs away from home, look forward to dinner out, having cocktails with friends, miss our family celebrations, are members of churches or volunteer organizations, and most of all, simply miss hugging our family and friends.

For three weeks, I couldn't bear to write fiction, even though I have a summer contract for the fifth novel in my Coconuts series. Since my writing contains a great deal of humor, I found it hard to find the funny during the pandemic. Until I thought of compiling this Quarantine Cookbook, I sat on my couch and watched news briefing after news briefing, becoming more anxious each day, as I'm sure you can relate.

This cookbook is helping me cope as much as I hope it helps you in the kitchen and elsewhere. Following are several activities that might get your mind off this chaotic crisis while we're all homebound:

1. Play your favorite music. It's an automatic mood booster.

2. Sing loudly, even if you sing off-key like me.

3. Dance in your living room. Not only will you get an immediate rush of good endorphins, you'll also get some welcome exercise.

4. Read! What better time to escape to a fictional world with a guaranteed happily ever after (or a happily for now.)

5. Take your camera into your yard and photograph birds, trees, flowers, clouds, or whatever catches your interest. Zoom in, zoom out. Who knows? You may become an amateur photographer.

6. Organize your computer files. Okay, this isn't fun but would fill several days.

7. Upload photos to your computer. Again, not fun but satisfying afterward.

8. Paint with your fingers. I guarantee this will put a smile on your face.

9. Blow bubbles. I mean, is it possible to blow bubbles without smiling? If you don't have actual store-bought bubbles, make some with dish soap and water.

10. Take a solitary walk in your yard and neighborhood, especially on sunny days. Bright sunshine brightens your mood unless you're a pluviophile who prefers rainy days.

11. Sit in your backyard and listen to the sounds of chirping birds. Try to identify them.

12. Make a pitcher of lemonade or take a cup of coffee or chilled glass of wine outside. Take the time to study flowers, trees, and the clouds. Remember when we were kids and noticed clouds that looked like puppies and unicorns? Bring back that joyful time.

13. Grab a hula hoop and time yourself. Try to improve your time or have contests with other members in your household. I promise it'll make you laugh as well as provide exercise.

14. Sidewalk chalk, anyone? Who doesn't love drawing flowers, smiley faces, dinosaurs, self-portraits, or whatever. After your kids have the fun, join in or better yet, draw a scene as a family. Dreaming of the beach? Start drawing waves, dolphins, and palm trees!

15. Paint your nails or toenails a funky color you wouldn't ordinarily use. After all, who will see them?!

16. Organize your spice drawer. I'm not kidding. It makes life much easier when you can quickly find the basil, chili

powder, paprika, poppy seeds, sage, or thyme. See how I did that in order? It's satisfying and will expedite your cooking.

17. Play board games and other activities for two or more (or play Solitaire alone.) I've always loved board games. My favorites are Dominoes, Scrabble, Yahtzee, and Guesstures. This is probably a very good time to play Monopoly since it takes so long. And who doesn't love the game we played as kids called Operation? Or Twister? That's sure to provide laughs.

18. Card games like Rook, Hearts, Spades, and Gin always provide giggles if you have at least two people in the house.

19. Complete a jigsaw puzzle. I admit I've never finished one but now seems like the perfect time to accomplish that goal.

20. My grandmother loved, loved, LOVED crossword puzzles. If you don't have any at home, there are plenty online. Just Google them. In addition to passing the time, you'll improve your vocabulary. Win-win.

21. Do something that shows immediate results. I find if I can actually see the results quickly, it boosts my mood. Some ideas include mowing the lawn, folding laundry, vacuuming, cleaning out a junk drawer, making the bed, doing dishes, or even coloring your own hair. It can be a one-hour task that will give you results for days.

22. Give your partner a massage; ask him or her to return the favor.

23. Trace your hand and pretend you're a kid again. Make something silly like a turkey or reindeer antlers.

24. Organize your closet. Make a donate pile for when you're able to actually go out and give to others.

25. Take up sketching even if you normally only draw stick figures or smiley faces. Focus on something of interest in your yard and begin with something simple like a planter or vase.

26. Now is a great time to journal. Keep track of meals you've made, how you and your family have handled this crisis, what activities have kept you busy, your feelings during the pandemic, and so on.

27. Make snow ice cream if you're in a cold, snowy state or country. I've included the recipe in this cookbook. It only takes a few ingredients and will make you feel like a kid again. Making this treat was a fun scene in my Christmas novella, MIRACLE ON AISLE TWO.

28. What better time to learn a foreign language than when you're quarantined. Check YouTube and Google for assistance.

29. If you're like me and your eyebrows are disappearing, study tutorials on how to create beautiful brows. Superfluous, I know, but it's something to do.

30. Be brave and try a Facebook live video. To be honest, I have yet to do this, and now my roots are showing, so if I do get up my courage to check in with readers, you can bet I'll be wearing a hat!

31. Get back to an old hobby. For me, that's piano playing. I hadn't touched my piano in fifteen years but did recently. I even posted the proof on my Facebook page. It was bad, by the way, but brought a much-needed laugh to many.

32. Support a non-profit that's aiding the cause.

33. Put a thank-you note in the mail box to thank your local mail carrier who has to touch everyone's germy mail.

34. Create signs or write notes of appreciation to local hospital employees, grocers, and trucking companies. They are

keeping this economy going, feeding us, and saving our lives. If you have kids at home, get out construction paper and crayons (or printer paper will do) and have them draw hearts and thank the same workers mentioned above.

35. Facetime with your family and friends. If you don't have an iPhone, try using the video option in Facebook messenger.

36. Find humor. I know that's extremely difficult during a pandemic, but I worked in marketing at two hospitals for over a decade. I once attended an in-service (workshop) on humor and wellness given by a nurse. Laughter is an important component of our wellbeing.

37. Watch Christmas movies or old black and white films.

38. Some people have strung holiday lights to perk up their mood and to show solidarity during this health epidemic. This will also help you find some inner joy.

39. Exercise: Walk, stretch, lift weights, box, dance, or take up yoga.

40. Binge watch your favorite television shows or discover a new series on Netflix.

41. Rearrange your bookshelf. Do you alphabetize by author or title? Maybe you put all of the thrillers on one shelf, romance on another, and self-help or non-fiction books on yet another row. I prefer this method so I can quickly read whatever genre I'm in the mood for.

42. Make masks if you're a seamstress. I can barely sew on a button, so I decided to create this cookbook instead.

43. Support local restaurants who offer curbside pickup and delivery.

44. Find joy by reading children's books. I love to read and write them. In fact, I've written four to date: WHAT DO YOU WANT TO BE?, THE MISSING KEY, SANTA'S

SECRET, and SOUR POWER.

45. Write an essay or article about your experience while in quarantine. How did you feel? What did you do to occupy yourself? What did you miss? What will you change once life gets back to normal? What did you eat? You get the idea.

46. Start a to-do, motivational jar. Write notes on small pieces of paper containing some of these tips or come up with your own.

47. If you have a kite, fly it in your back yard.

48. Try gardening. Either clean out big planters on your deck, or prepare a small section of your yard. Seeds may be ordered online. Don't forget to water them and enjoy your bounty in a few months.

49. Paint a room or an accent wall a cheery color.

50. Check on elderly parents, grandparents, and neighbors. Drop off groceries or medicine if you can.

51. Reach out via social media. I call it my water cooler as a writer, and now more than ever, we need to post news, upbeat stories, photos that will make others smile, and helpful tips.

52. Treat yourself to a relaxing bubble bath with soft music and candles.

53. Light candles even during the day. They're soothing, and eucalyptus is supposed to help with stress.

54. Color with your kids or even by yourself. It's therapeutic and fun. If you have a family member in a nursing home, this is a great way to show them love through the window.

55. If allowed in your city, build a small bon fire (on a non-windy day) and make s'mores using graham crackers, marshmallows, and chocolate.

56. Clean your windows, flower pots, and patio furniture so you'll be ready when it's safe to invite guests over for a cookout.

57. Get out of your pajamas, shower, wash your hair, and put on real clothes. You'll feel better even if no one else sees you.

58. Cook! Be sure and try some of these recipes and let me know which ones are your favorite. You can reach me through the contact page on my website: www.bethcarter.com

Six-Word Memoirs on Quarantine Life

Have you ever heard of six-word memoirs? I discovered them while reading a "101 Best Websites" by *Writer's Digest Magazine* years ago and I'm so glad I did. Since then, I've written a few hundred tiny memoirs and have been featured in two six-word memoir books and one six-word calendar, alongside celebrities and famous authors. Six-word memoirs are often poignant, funny, sad, compelling, and in this case, timely.

As background, Larry Smith, founder of *SMITH Magazine*, created the poignant sixer community in 2006. Since then, he has gotten tens of thousands of people hooked on them. Check out his site at www.sixwordmemoirs.com. I had the pleasure of meeting Larry during a six-word slam held at the 92nd Street Y in New York City. He's a great guy, by the way. Interesting side note: Larry happens to be married to Piper Kerman, author of Orange Is the New Black. I bet you learned something new today!

How it all originated: Six-word memoirs allegedly began when Ernest Hemingway was challenged to write a story using only six words. Here's his infamous six-word memoir:

For sale: Baby shoes. Never worn.

This is a great writing form during quarantine because it's quick and there's no right or wrong except for one rule: use only six words that pack a punch. Also, use punctuation to your advantage. Here are several memoirs I wrote about life in quarantine:

COVID-19: Scariest time of my life.

Don't hoard. Leave something for everyone.

Healthcare workers are heroes; thank you.

Virus doesn't discriminate--rich, poor. Vulnerable.

The Class of 2020 got screwed.

Embrace quirkiness. You're alone, yet not.

Be kind. No time for jerks.

Social media becomes a loyal friend.

Find joy doing fun, simple tasks.

PLAY GAMES, DANCE, SING, READ, COOK.

Toilet paper hoarders, one word: Karma.

Binge watch television shows and movies.

Manage stress. Do favorite things inside.

Breathe. Exhale. This pandemic will end.

Writing novels from home. Prefer Starbucks.

Stay informed. Don't overload on news.

Organize, nap, exercise, read, and repeat.

Brother is a flight nurse. Praying.

New terms: Social distance. Flatten curve.

Help others. Drop off groceries, medications.

Can't wait to hug my parents.

World upside down. Birds still singing.

Priorities shift to family, love, patience.

Remember, this will pass. It's temporary.

Face mask equals weird tan lines.

Future plans: Stock coffee, wine. Repeat.

I wonder how gray I'll get.

Would you choose different quarantine partner?

COVID-19: Horror movie with invisible monster.

2020 BROUGHT TO YOU BY HITCHCOCK.

Aren't six-word memoirs unique? They're therapeutic too. As you can see, they can be funny, sad, thoughtful, and powerful. Try writing some of your own. Get your family involved (even from afar.) I'd love to hear yours. In fact, go to www.sixwordmemoirs.com and submit your own. They're holding a contest on pandemic memoirs as of this writing.

Other Books By The Author

Novels

THURSDAYS AT COCONUTS (Book 1)

CHAOS AT COCONUTS (Book 2)

BABIES AT COCONUTS (Book 3)

COWBOYS AT COCONUTS (Book 4)

BRIDES AT COCONUTS (Book 5 – coming in 2020)

One final novel (Book 6) will complete this series in 2021.

Don't miss these multi-award-winning novels.

SLEEPING WITH ELVIS

MIRACLE ON AISLE TWO, a holiday novella

SANTA BABY (a novelette in the anthology, SIZZLE IN THE SNOW)

Children's Picture Books

WHAT DO YOU WANT TO BE?

THE MISING KEY

SANTA'S SECRET

SOUR POWER

My novels are available through Amazon or Barnes & Noble as both paperbacks or eBooks (free with Kindle Unlimited!) My children's books are paperback only and are illustrated beautifully. Two are written in verse and two are not. Find my books on my Amazon author page at:

www.amazon.com/author/bethcarter

Let's Connect

Now more than ever, it's important to have social connections. Since we can't leave our houses as of this writing, we can still maintain a connection via Facebook, Twitter, Instagram, Zoom, and other social media. You'll find me most days on at least one of these platforms—usually Facebook—where I spend far too much time. I love interacting with readers.

BookBub:

https://www.bookbub.com/authors/beth-carter

Facebook:

https://www.facebook.com/authorbethcarter

Twitter:

https://twitter.com/bethcarter007

Instagram:

https://www.instagram.com/bethcarterauthor

Amazon Author Page:

http://amazon.com/author/bethcarter

BETH'S BOOK BABES

I have a private reader group on Facebook and would love to have you join us. Members of Beth's Book Babes get the first scoop on my writing projects, participate in contests to name characters, receive sneak peeks of cover reveals, discuss reading and writing, and more. It's easy to join. Simply request an invitation to join *Beth's Book Babes* on Facebook or let me know via the contact page on my website, **www.bethcarter.com**

Author Bio

After being a bank vice president and a hospital public relations director, Beth Carter shed her suits and heels to reinvent herself at a certain mid-life age. While drinking copious amounts of coffee, she has penned: THURSDAYS AT COCONUTS, CHAOS AT COCONUTS, BABIES AT COCONUTS, COWBOYS AT COCONUTS, SLEEPING WITH ELVIS, MIRACLE ON AISLE TWO, and SANTA BABY, a novelette.

Carter is a multi-award-winning author of a 2015 RONE Award, named Best Debut Author in 2015, a 2017 & 2018 RAVEN Award runner-up for Favorite Contemporary, as well as a 2019 finalist and is a 2020 RONE nominee.

The author also writes children's picture books including WHAT DO YOU WANT TO BE?, SOUR POWER, THE MISSING KEY, and SANTA'S SECRET. Additionally, her work appears in four six-word memoir collections and numerous anthologies.

Splitting her time between Missouri and Florida, Beth Carter is often found writing at Starbucks—if she isn't shopping at T.J. Maxx, boating, or watching deer in her backyard.

A Note from the Author

I hope you've enjoyed THE QUARANTINE COOKBOOK. Even though I've written ten books—six novels and four children's picture books—this is my first ever non-fiction book. I wrote and compiled it in record time—two weeks. I couldn't have been happier to have a project during quarantine and am eager to donate the proceeds to Tunnel2Towers.org, which has always supported families of fallen first responders and are now doing the same for families of healthcare workers who sadly lost their battle to COVID-19.

None of us will likely ever forget the Coronavirus pandemic of 2020. After all, it's still an ongoing (as of this moment) worldwide health crisis that caught most countries off guard. I hope we're all able to go about our normal routines soon.
Meanwhile, cooking is a great distraction and your family will thank you. I can't wait to hear which recipes become your favorites. Please feel free to email me via my website at

www.bethcarter.com and share photos. I've created the hashtags:

#TheQuarantineCookbook and **#thequarantinecookbook**

so we can all enjoy them.

Again, thank you for your support. Please stay safe, healthy, and remember this pandemic *is* temporary.

Warmly,

Beth Carter, Author

Index